Grief By Day

GINA PEOTTER

BALBOA.PRESS
A DIVISION OF HAY HOUSE

Balboa Press books may be ordered through booksellers or by contacting:

Balboa Press
A Division of Hay House
1663 Liberty Drive
Bloomington, IN 47403
www.balboapress.com
844-682-1282

Print information available on the last page.

ISBN: 978-1-9822-7696-6 (sc)
ISBN: 978-1-9822-7697-3 (e)

Balboa Press rev. date: 05/27/2022

This book is dedicated to all the grieving souls I have crossed paths with in my life. *You* are the reason why I wrote this book. Every experience and conversation has made me into who I am today. I have learned so much from each of you.

This book is also dedicated to each of you reading this book who is trusting in the words of this book to provide healing. I trust in the universe that this book will touch many lives and help many more!

Lastly, my family: my oldest daughter asked if I was dedicating this book to her … I told her it was dedicated to our dog Leo instead. In all seriousness, she is always an amazing sounding board and rational advice giver at the young age of twelve. Also to my husband, who goes along on this crazy ride of life, and my youngest daughter, who shows me the world through a happy and goofy lens. As well as my sisters who walked through this grief roller coaster together, and my extended family and friends. You are my world. I am grateful for you all every day.

Welcome

I am so glad you took the step to see how you can move forward in your healing journey. This book was created to reach *more* people where they are and at their own pace, in hopes of *more* people healing and growing in their grief journey. Grief is not something to get over or something that needs fixing, but with the right tools it can make your healing journey healthier and more meaningful.

This book is intended for anyone who has gone through the death of a friend or family member.

Grief By Day is broken into two sections, taking grief day by day or by month. You choose. Sometimes, in grief, even taking things a day at a time can be hard. If you can work your way up to taking life by the day or the month, you are stepping in the right direction.

First Section: 90 Days of Reflection

Each day is broken into two parts. They are labeled "First Year" for anyone who had a death within the past 356 days. "Year +" is intended for anyone past the year mark after a death. I'm not implying there is a time limit on grief, but most people's lives look a bit different days or weeks after a death versus one year or five-plus years later.

How to Use This Section

You can use the 90 days any way you would like.

- Follow along and start at day one.
- Open it up and pick a day to start at.
- Read a few all at once and ponder the questions.
- Take a few minutes each week to go through one day.
- I have seen people turn this into a book club as well. Each week go through five days on your own; then meet to talk through your actions and answers.
- Read them together with a trusted friend, and share your thoughts.
- Use this section as journaling prompts, get out a journal, notebook, paper or computer and write out your thoughts. See where the prompts may take you.

This is designed to work any way you want it to. *The goal is to be true to yourself and hopefully heal in the process.*

Second Section: Monthly Exercises

Each month has its own theme along with some educational pieces, mixed in with some of my own personal stories and encounters with others going through a death. There is an action item at the end of each month listed. Again, this can be done any way you would like, alone or with a friend or group. *The goal is to be true to yourself and hopefully heal in the process.*

From the Author

I believe in trying different things and seeing what helps and what doesn't, and then coming back and trying it again at a different point in my life. If you are open and honest, this book will help you work through some tough topics.

After I lost my parents when I was in my twenties, my life completely changed. I've also lost my grandparents, lots of aunts and uncles, friends, and pets. I dealt with it all by holding everything inside for a long time. It wasn't until I struggled with massive anxiety, major depression, and constant suicidal thoughts that I started working through my grief. Those seasons in my life were like a roller coaster, just like the journey of grief. My hope for you is that you work through your grief before it takes you to a dark place the way mine did.

This book is a compilation of struggles I've worked through and topics I see over and over with adults I work with who are grieving. For many of us who were taught to keep our emotions at bay or feel "crazy" because our emotions are all over the place … this book is for you. Honesty will be your best friend throughout this book. If you can really be truthful to what it is that is going on, you have the power to heal through it. *You got this; I believe in you!*

Contents

MONTHLY EXERCISES

90 Days
of Reflection

Day 1

First Year

Don't let it break you. No matter how difficult things seem right now, life will go on, and you will survive.

—Stay Strong

You might be at the point where things seem fine, but then a song, picture, or piece of clothing will trigger your grief again. You will survive and can move past these grief triggers when the time is right. If you ask the question "What is this trying to teach me right now?" you move from a mindset of being a victim of your circumstance to a growth mindset.

Q: Think back to the last time you had a difficult situation. What was it trying to teach you?

Year +

I don't want to stay stuck here. I don't want to live the rest of my days as a shell of myself. I don't want to ignore pain because ignoring pain means missing out on joy.

—Laura Jack

That is a powerful quote. Some people don't realize they are walking through life numb and ignoring the pain because it's tough. By pushing down your feelings for days, months, and years, it might mean you are missing out on joy in your life. Take some time today to reflect on what you are actually doing with your feelings.

Q: Are you ignoring your pain?

Day 2

First Year

Feelings are just visitors, let them come and go.

—Mooji

That can be scary for some people. Letting yourself cry when the feeling arises can be tough. If you have not let your feelings come and go as they pop up, you might not know what to do with them. It's like retraining your brain to feel those feelings. It is going to take time.

Some people have the opposite issue—constant emotions and crying. Wrangling in your emotions as they come can be a task that you are not used to either. This will come with practice. It may not be centered completely around grief, but starting with working on feelings in general is a step in the right direction.

Q: *What are you feeling right now?* Work on labeling your feelings as a first step.

Year +

You cannot change what you refuse to confront.

—Unknown

Mic drop! If deep down you know you have an alcohol problem but don't want to do anything about it, you will never change. If deep down you know you are having an issue with the death of someone but do not want to call a counselor or seek help—well, I'm sorry to tell you, but nothing will change unless you make the effort.

Q: *Truthfully, what is something that you really don't want to confront?*

Day 3

First Year

You cannot heal a lifetime of pain overnight, be patient with yourself, it takes as long as it takes to rebuild yourself.

—livehappy.com

I love and dislike this quote so much. It makes complete sense, but at the same time, I just want to push the fast-forward button to make myself feel better.

Q: What do you wish you could push the fast-forward button for? What would be the downfall of doing so?

Year +

There is nothing I want more than to fall asleep and wake up to find it's all just been a bad dream.

—Joy's Mental Health Mission

Wouldn't that be great if you could wake up and have everything be back to "normal"? Let's go with that for a minute. What would you do this week with the person who died if he or she were still alive? What would be different today about your everyday life? Take some time to think about how much has changed in your life since your loved one died.

Q: What in your life has been positive since the death of your loved one?

Day 4

First Year

The struggle you're in today is developing the strength you need for tomorrow.

—Unknown

It can be hard to look at tough struggles as a positive aspect for your life. Take some time to think through past struggles and reflect on what strength you gained from them.

Q: What do you see your current struggle as—a lesson, an opportunity for growth, your destiny, or just a problem?

Year +

I have endured, I have been broken, I have known hardship, I have lost myself. But here I stand, still moving forward, growing stronger each day.

—Tiny Buddha

Reflecting on how much you have grown, changed, and learned over the last year is something that might provide you with some clarity. Remind yourself that you have come a long way.

Q: What has been the biggest thing you have learned in the past year?

Day 5

First Year

Your wound is probably not your fault, but your healing is your responsibility.

—Denice Frohman

You are the only one who can choose to make your life happier or better. Your healing is your responsibility, not the responsibility of your spouse, parent, or counselor. It is up to you to choose to make better choices, use better words, have better reactions to situations, or develop healthier habits.

Q: What have you not taken responsibility for in the past?

Year +

And to my grief I am grateful for those hours of recollection … even the moments that simultaneously shattered and healed my heart.

—Steady and Flight

There is some power in finding gratitude in tough times. It shows that you are in control of your happiness and are taking power over your feelings. A death is a horrible, terrible thing that can shatter many souls, but how you approach your healing can make a world of difference.

Q: What are five things you are grateful for today?

Day 6

First Year

Don't miss out on something that could be amazing just because it could also be difficult.

—Live Life Happy

I keep coming back to this quote, but it is on purpose. Change is difficult. Death is difficult. Healing can be difficult. That is the reason why a lot of people don't move forward through grief. But difficult things can turn into something amazing. Amazing new relationships, amazing healing, amazing better feelings in our bodies and minds.

Q: Would you be happy with your life if how you felt today was how you felt the rest of your life?

Year +

Some people may not understand why those grieving are reluctant to move into a new year. For them they see a fresh year, a new season … but for the bereaved it's moving into a new calendar year, which their loved one will never live in.

—Zoe Clark-Coates

Starting something new without the person who died can be tough. You know this firsthand: your mom, brother, sister, son, or grandma is not there to walk through life with you. It might not seem fair that others get to have their mom, brother, sister, son, or grandma in their lives, and they don't cherish time with them.

I struggled with this for a long time after my dad died. Friends would talk about not wanting to go home from college for Father's Day because something fun was going on at the college campus. To me it was a slap in the face. I couldn't go home to see my dad, and everyone else was complaining about going to see theirs. I now realize that people are living in their own realities or worlds with their cares, and I was internalizing those comments based on my current reality.

Q: What about other people's comments or actions made you upset after the death?

Day 7

First Year

Fill your heart with gratitude and joy. There is still so much beauty and goodness in this world.

—Unknown

Sometimes it can be hard to think about gratitude when you are grieving the loss of a friend or family member.

A five-minute daily gratitude journal can increase long-term well-being by 10%.

—Halo Recognition

A good structure for writing out gratitude is to say what you are grateful for. Think about life if you did not have that thing—what that would feel like? Write down why you are grateful for that thing, and really think about it. Then say "thank you" with lots of appreciation. Doing this small exercise can cause you to think about the reason why it matters and really show appreciation for the thing you are grateful for. It might look something like this:

I am grateful for _____ because _____.
Thank you!

Q: What are five things you are truly grateful for today?

Year +

> There are moments which mark your life; moments when you realize nothing will ever be the same and time is divided into two parts: *before* and *after* this.
>
> —Unknown

There is a dividing line in your life before death and after. You might have been on a wild journey through life since the death of your loved one. Keeping memories alive can be therapeutic for some. Take some time this week to think of (or research) a way you can do something in memory of your loved one.

- Have a bench made at your local park in memory of the person who died.
- Plant a tree in memory of your loved one.
- Have a bear or quilt made out of their old clothing.
- Light a candle in memory of your person and look at old photos.
- Donate to their favorite charity or a group that specializes in the ailment they died from.
- Write on an online tribute wall in memory of the person who died.
- Share memories of your loved one with another friend or family member.

Q: What will you do this week?

Day 8

First Year

You don't "get over" losing a child, you just get to a point where your head and your heart come to an understanding of how much pain and sadness you can live with.

—Kane

Wow! This can be true for any type of loss. I always say you can't get over a death, but you can heal your wounds. Sadness might always be there in your heart, but you may come to a point where you live with it and learn how to heal yourself bit by bit.

Q: How do you describe grief to other people?

Year +

Time will pass anyway. You can either spend it creating the life you want or spend it living the life you don't want. The choice is yours.

—Unknown

Life moves fast and slow at the same time. Oftentimes people are caught up in the day-in-and-day-out tasks and work. Then one day you wake up and realize something you were thinking about was a year or two ago already.

Fear is usually the robber of dreams, actions, and trying new things. If you could cast away your fears about moving forward in your grief journey, or something specific in life … what would you do?

Q: How would you feel about your life if today was your last day, and you looked back at all you have done (or not done)?

Day 9

First Year

My husband died. I don't need advice. All I need is for you to gently close your mouth, open wide your heart, and walk with me, until I can see in color again.

—Unknown

Holy man, I love this. Yes, it is bold, but it rings true for a lot of people who have gone through the death of someone. What most people say they really needed at the time of death was someone to just be there … not to give advice, but just be there. Some of us have a hard time knowing that is what we need, or have a hard time asking for help or a companion. It is tough. It stinks, but getting clear with what you need can be helpful, even years after the death of your loved one.

Q: What do you need today?

Year +

Sometimes you don't realize the weight of something you've been carrying until you feel the weight of its release.

—Power of Positivity

Many people are carrying really heavy things around all day and don't even realize it. It could be something big like guilt or shame, or even chronic stress. Those things are heavy. So is grief. Pushing your feelings down can make them extremely heavy. People sometimes realize what they are carrying is so heavy when they break down crying, or have a large anger fit over something … it isn't until those emotions are revealed that they realize how much they haven't dealt with or were carrying.

Q: If you could label something heavy in your life, what would it be? How would it feel to get rid of it forever … or even for a little while?

Day 10

First Year

Perhaps the butterfly is proof that you can go through a great deal of darkness and still become something beautiful.

—Tiny Buddha

Some of the most wonderful people I have met in my life have been ones with a very damaged or hurt soul. This was because of things such as death, abuse, depression, and many dark days. The reason I share this with you is to let you know it is possible to come out on the other side of a tragedy and dark mind. Your time on this earth can be happy and joyful; it is possible.

Q: What have you been keeping inside that you wish people understood?

Year +

You can close the door on grief, but it will peek in through the window.

—Unknown

This is so true. I tried it for years. What I didn't realize was that it would cause me to have panic attacks and anxiety attacks down the road after not dealing with my strong emotions. (I'm not saying this will happen to you; it is just what happened with my life). This quote actually came from the book *Grieving Dads: To the Brink and Back*. It is a fantastic book written by dads for dads. I highly recommend reading this book even if you aren't a dad; it rings true to the raw emotions and actions people go through after a tough death.

Q: What is something you will explore this week that you have not done yet related to grief and healing?

- Read a grief book or personal development book.
- Listen to a podcast.

- Join a grief group.
- Write a letter to the person who died.
- Connect with a counselor/professional.
- Take a relaxation class of some kind.
- Reach out to a person who also lost a friend/family member.
- Dig out those old videos or movies you have been unable to watch -Let yourself cry, be sad, be joyful ….

Day 11

First Year

One small crack does not mean that you are broken, it means that you were put to the test and you didn't fall apart.

—Linda Pointexter

You might have a crack or a hundred in your heart, but that doesn't mean you are completely broken. Those cracks show that you didn't fall apart, and maybe you are mending them together as the days go on or as you work through your grief. That ache is proof that you are living through it each day.

Q: What is the biggest source of your strength? What gets you through the tough times?

Year +

We all have a bag. We all pack differently. Some of us are traveling light. Some of us are secret hoarders who've never parted with a memory in our lives. I think we are all called to figure out how to carry our bag to the best of our ability, how to unpack it, and how to face the mess. I think part of growing up is learning how to sit down on the floor with all your things and figure out what to take with you and what to leave behind.

—Hannah Brencher

Working through "unpacking" your grief or feelings may sound overwhelming to some people. What do you do to process these emotions, or where do you turn? This goes back to the beginning of your grief: most people do not have previous experience or knowledge in where to get grief resources. Really, why would you if you hadn't gone through a loss before?

Q: What are your next steps in your healing journey? Be sure to take action with resources available to you: rent a book, view a video, or talk to someone who will lend a nonjudgmental ear. Call your local funeral home and ask for some resources; search for grief support in your area. Take the Grief Your Way assessment to get a tailored grief plan for you (www.griefyourway.com) *You are responsible for your own healing,* but don't forget there are many resources out there for you if you choose to look.

Day 12

First Year

Be not afraid of growing slowly, be afraid only of standing still.

—Chinese Proverb

What would it feel like to look back on today five years from now and realize you are stuck in the same mindset and have never felt any better than today? If you are struggling right now, that would be pretty discouraging to look back five years and realize you lived your life in the same pain for *five* years! That is the reality for some people: they stand still for years and don't even know it. They don't work on getting better or try to improve themselves and heal.

Q: Take a step back from your life. How would you truthfully describe your current situation (mental health, physical health, grief journey, etc.)?

Year +

It's okay if you thought you were over it, but it hits you all over again. It's okay to fall apart even after you thought you had it under control. You are not weak, healing is messy. And there is no timeline for healing.

—Unknown

Grief is a crazy thing. Life sometimes gets in the way of *really* letting a person process grief. It may hit you when you least expect it. Some people describe it as waves or as a roller coaster.

Q: What is the best way you describe grief to someone else? Is there an analogy or metaphor that you resonate with that describes grief as a picture?

Day 13

First Year

Stop holding on to what hurts, and start making room for what feels good.

—Unknown

This quote is great for many reasons. To some people it can sound selfish, especially if your loss is really recent. Why should I feel joy when there is a massive hole in my life and the world? And to others there might be a huge sense of guilt surrounding that statement—why do I deserve to be happy? People might think I'm not actually sad. Life is short, and you know this firsthand. If there are moments when you can let some joy into your life, give it a whirl. You are worth some joy after a large amount of sadness.

Q: What could you do for five or ten minutes today that would bring you some joy?

Year +

Healing doesn't mean the damage never existed.

—Unknown

Shattered hearts still beat strongly. Moving forward does not mean you are not honoring your loved one. You have gone through something horrible, but that doesn't mean that you are damaged goods. Many people in this world are also going through a terrible death. Do you ever think about what would happen if you didn't go forward in your healing journey? Moving forward can be slow because we don't realize we have improved. Life can grow so busy getting through each day that we are unaware that we are our own worst enemy, stopping ourselves from getting better.

Q: What would happen if your current state did stay in your current state forever? What would happen if your state on the day your loved one died was your current state right now? What is the cost in your life of not going forward in your grief journey?

Day 14

First Year

It's not what you look at that matters, it's what you see.

—Henry David Thoreau

If two people watch a storm, one person might think about how beautiful the rain is on the water; the other person might be terrified and worried about the wind. It is how you choose to look at things that reflects your outlook and attitude. Take some time today to purposely look at nature and be in awe of the beauty of the creation around you.

Q: What was something amazing you saw in nature today?

Year +

They don't understand pain because their world didn't stop when ours did.

—Unknown

Others may not understand how you are feeling or what is going on in your mind. Others did not walk in your shoes. Others are not dealing with your reality or missing that exact person as they were to you. It is okay to be bitter toward others as you see them move on, and you are still struggling inside, one year later or thirty or more years later. Grief is tough. Nobody asked to go through the death of someone close to them.

"As human beings, we *love* to avoid things that are difficult and tough to feel. This means we often do everything in our power to stop, avoid, or numb difficult emotions. We keep ourselves busy to ignore them, we use drugs or alcohol to numb ourselves to them, or we find other ways to avoid them. Problem is, when we try to avoid thoughts, it actually hurts our overall mental health and well-being instead of helping it.

"Now it is important to note here that positive emotions absolutely help and improve our mental health. But that doesn't mean we should strive to only feel positive emotions while we try to stuff or numb the negative ones" (*What's Your Grief*).

Q: What negative thoughts or emotions do you still have around the death(s) or about your grief? Make a list or mental note. Remember, you can always rip up the list, burn it, or type it out and delete it; this exercise is meant to help you and for you to be *truthful* to yourself about your feelings.

Day 15

First Year

All you need is one safe anchor to keep you grounded when the rest of your life spins out of control.

—Katie Kacvinsky

Being grounded can take on many meanings. In this context we are talking about keeping you in check, or bringing you back to your core beliefs and values. Is there anything that you do to keep yourself grounded? If you have one person, one form of healing, one form of coping, or one form of grounding, you can start there.

Q: What is one way you are coping that is healthy? What is one way you are coping that is unhealthy?

Year +

They said: "Write the longest sentence you know." I wrote: "A life without you."

—Cameron Lincoln

Maybe you are at peace with your life right now. Maybe you are not; either way, let's daydream for a bit. What would your life look like today if that person(s) were still alive?

Q: How old would they be? What would celebrating their birthday (or anniversary) be like this year? What activities would you share with them this week? How would they fit into your everyday life again? What do you think their outlook would be on the current state of the world? *What would their other family members or friends be doing with them?*

Day 16

First Year

> Community is about sharing my life about allowing chaos of another's circumstances to infringe on mine; about permitting myself to be known without constraint; about resigning myself to needing others.

> —Sandy Oshiro Rosen

Think about sharing your life with others. This might be something therapeutic if you have been closing yourself off to the world after death. This can be done in online groups—either a grief group or some type of hobby you enjoy, or even an in-person grief group or meetup. If you don't feel comfortable sharing your life with people you don't know, think of your inner community—friends, coworkers, neighbors, and family that you have been closing off. Start by writing a letter; you don't have to share this if you don't want to.

Q: Who can you connect with this week?

Year +

> Being a good mother while my world fell apart was the hardest role I've ever played.

> —Unknown

Some of you may be navigating your own grief and helping children or others move through theirs as well. That is tough. Some people put others' needs first before their own. Being conscious of your needs or avoidances is huge. Check out this snippet from an article on avoidance through What's Your Grief:

What does avoidance look like?

- Isolation or withdrawing from others
- Staying busy or occupied

- Avoidance of people, places, and activities out of fear of grief being triggered
- Avoidance of feelings and emotions
- Substance use or abuse
- Acting as though everything is fine
- Avoidance of movies you know will make you cry or feel strong emotions

Q: When was the last time you met a tough feeling head on? Maybe you were afraid of something but did it anyway. Maybe you hesitated to take action about getting help in your grief journey but made the call anyway. *One action item for this week is to move through a tough feeling/emotion and make note of how it felt to be on the other side.*

Day 17

First Year

The weird, weird thing about devastating loss is that life actually goes on. When you're faced with a tragedy, a loss so huge that you have no idea how you can live through it, somehow, the world keeps turning, the seconds keep ticking.

—James Patterson

I've used this quote often, and it rings true to me every time. I think back to the death of my dad, and I couldn't understand how people were at work or kids in school when there was a massive hole in this world and my heart. Your world stops, but everyone else keeps going. You just went through such deep pain. The checkout lady at Kohl's when I was buying my funeral dress had no stinking clue what I had just gone through!

Q: What was the most shocking thing to you after the death of your person(s)?

Year +

I can wipe away the tears from my eyes. But ... I can't wipe away the pain in my heart.

—all-greatquotes.com

Doing things in memory of our loved ones can bring comfort for some of us. Visiting a gravesite alone or with others brings comfort to some people. Donating money to a charity for the person who died can be a great way to honor places or organizations they loved. Planting a memory tree at a public park or in your backyard or at your cabin is another great idea. Some have also had benches made or purchased at community gardens, or stones engraved.

Q: What ideas can you think of to honor your loved one?

Ask others what they have done to commemorate or honor their loved one. If you don't know anyone who has gone through a death, look online, or try one of the ideas mentioned. Take note of how it made you feel, what emotions came up when doing the act of memories.

Day 18

First Year

When you arise in the morning, think of what precious privilege it is to be alive—to breathe, to think, to enjoy, to love.

—Marcus Aurelius

You might know this more than some people: life can be taken away from you in an instant, and tomorrow is not guaranteed. This goes back to the topic of gratitude—take some time to think about what you really are grateful for. Nearly 150,000 people die in the world each day ….

Q: What can you do today or tomorrow to show gratitude for your life?

Year +

No rule book. No time frame. No judgment. Grief is an individual as a fingerprint. Do what is right for your soul.

—lfw

Some people feel as if they are missing the magic book or road map on how to navigate the grief, sadness, loss, guilt … all the emotions and situations. Sorry to say, there is no magic book (well, maybe this one). *But* by being open to new experiences, healing ideas, and options, you are making an effort to work through your healing journey, and that is progress.

Every person, situation, relationship, and death is different, and that is a beautiful thing.

Q: What made your relationship with the person who died so special? Or if it was not a good relationship, what made it so difficult? Write it down, talk it out, type it out, think it through; any way you process it is okay, but be honest with yourself.

Day 19

First Year

One of the most cathartic practices is to talk about the loss, but many people don't speak up because they fear no one really wants to hear the details of how they're feeling.

—forevermissed.com

Some people may feel like a burden talking to others about death and how they are doing. Others may not feel that anyone can actually relate to what they are going through, so it doesn't even pay to bring it up. Grief is a tricky topic in our society. Some people are very open about it, but most tend to be awkward if they have not gone through a death before. This can add a layer of difficulty to a person trying to move forward in their grieving journey.

Q: Have you been quiet about what you really are going through over the last year(s)? What would help you right now? Set a timer for two minutes, and think through this question. Feel free to write anything down that comes to mind, but it's not necessary.

Year +

Start before you are ready.

—Steven Pressfield

This can be truthful for many things, but in relation to healing and grief, it seems spot on. Nobody wants to walk down that hospital hallway to identify their loved one. Nobody wants to actually see their wife in a casket. Nobody wants to pick out burial clothes for their child. Nobody wants to step up to a counter and purchase a grief book to read. Nobody wants to tell a story about how their mom died.

What all those people have in common is they did it—they took a step, whether it was out of obligation, force, or the way things had to happen—and they took a step in their healing, whether they knew it or not. Sometimes that's where people stop taking steps. "The obligatory funeral is done, and I don't have to deal with this anymore. I will stuff my feelings down, avoid crying, and life will go on." What some do not understand is that others are taking steps, going to grief groups or working on their tough stuff by talking to others, journaling, or calling a counselor, and are step by step moving forward. And most of those people took a step before they were ready.

Q: What could you do this week to take a step before you are ready?

Day 20

First Year

> In any given moment we have two options: to step forward into growth or step back into safety.

> —Abraham Maslow

Even though you may have heard this before, it is a good reminder. By not taking a step forward, you might be sitting in the safe zone. And sometimes in life that might serve you a purpose, such as right after a death, a trauma, or a transitional season in your life. Take time to think about what season of your life you are in right now.

Q: What if you took a step forward? What concerns do you have, and what would things look like if it helped you feel better?

Year +

> You can't be committed to your own bullshit and to your growth. It's one or the other.

> —Scott Stabile

Do you tell yourself (and maybe others) a story about what is going on in your life? If you really look at the story you are telling yourself, are you playing the victim card, or placing a lot of guilt on yourself for something? Examining the story you tell yourself can open your eyes to what you are making yourself believe. If you are committed to growth and feeling better in your grief journey, take time to *truthfully* look at what you are repeating over and over as your "story."

Many people in grief tell themselves the story that nobody can relate to what is going on. Nobody else feels this bad. If you really are in a tough mental space, please reach out to a professional. Acting now will help in the long run. A lot of behavioral health places in the United States schedule appointments six weeks to twelve months out. That's a long time to wait when you are not in a good mental space. I remember calling to schedule an appointment with a psychologist, and they told me the next available appointment was twelve months out. Talk about feeling helpless. If that is you, just keep trying. You can ask your doctor for a referral. There are places that can get you in. Step one is being honest with yourself.

Q: What is the story you tell yourself surrounding the death of your loved one?

Day 21

First Year

We meet no ordinary people in our lives.

—C. S. Lewis

We don't always stop to think about what makes someone stand out, yet each person brings something special to the table. What is unique about you? Take a moment today and celebrate both of you.

Q: What was the most unique thing about your loved one?

Year +

We begin to remember not just that you died, but that you lived. And that your life gave us memories too beautiful to forget.

—Unknown

Have you reached a point where you are looking to celebrate the life of your loved one? There are always times when looking at photos or talking about the person who died will help. If you can smile while telling a funny story, or not cry or be angry while talking about a past memory, that is a step in the right direction.

Q: What is one memory of your loved one that not many others know about or were there for? If you feel comfortable, share that memory with someone.

Day 22

First Year

Starting today, I need to forget what's gone, appreciate what still remains, and look forward to what's coming next.

—Unknown

Having something to look forward to is an important part of healing. Make a plan—whether it's having lunch with a friend or a zoom date with a friend or family member, sighing up for an online class, picking up a make-and-take project from the art store, renting a new movie you have been waiting to watch, ordering or renting a new book, booking a trip for a special occasion (or no occasion at all), or planning to try food from a new restaurant—that allows you to look forward rather than constantly looking back.

Q: What can you do this week that will provide you with some excitement or joy?

Year +

Don't live in the past, thinking about mistakes or changes you made. Think of your life as a book, move forward, close one chapter and open another. Learn from your mistakes, but focus on your future, not on your past.

—Unknown

Moving forward in your life can be tough. It may seem as though you are leaving the person who died behind, and you are not honoring them by mourning them. Think about it on the flip side: if someone close to you was struggling with your death, would you want them to be going through a tough time or living life and enjoying it?

Q: What can you do to lift any burdens about the death? Seek out a counselor, meditate, visit a grave, journal, talk to someone—?

Day 23

First Year

Never regret a day in your life. Good days give you happiness and bad days give you experience. Both are essential in life.

—Anonymous

It is easy to look back and wish you had made different choices. "If only I had done this or said that." You can only live in the moment and do your best today.

Q: What "should haves" and "could haves" are you hanging on to?

Year +

After a trauma you feel frozen in time and disconnected to everyone and everything including yourself it seems to take forever to re-connect and become alive again.

—tanjawindegger.com

Some people feel like there is a before and after—a life before the death, and now the after. Walking through life can be a difficult dance. It might seem that not many people can relate to what you went through and are living with today. But you can take control of your healing.

Q: Have you celebrated how far you have come? From that day one to now, what have you worked through? What have you learned? Take some time to *really* reflect on where you are now.

Day 24

First Year

Be kind, for everyone you meet is fighting a hard battle.

—Plato

When you are feeling sad and overwhelmed, it sometimes appears that everyone else is happy and content. In fact, everyone has their own struggles. While it may not be grief, what they are facing can be equally tough to bear. Most people put on a mask to hide their sadness, and you may be doing so to a certain degree as well.

Be good to the people you meet. Show them compassion, knowing that they too have sadness to bear. Nothing takes you out of your own thoughts of sadness like the joy that comes from doing something for someone else. Make time today to show kindness to someone in your life.

Q: What can you do to reach out to someone or offer up some kindness?

Year +

Grieving is like having broken ribs. On the outside, you look fine, but with every breath, it hurts.

—forevermissed.com

Holding feelings inside is something many people do. Most people put on a façade and act like everything is okay. Usually people do this to protect others—kids, or the feelings of family members or friends—or not to talk more about their feelings.

Q: What would you really *say to someone if they asked how you are doing?*

Day 25

First Year

That was the hard thing about grief, and the grieving. They spoke another language, and the words we knew always fell short of what we wanted them to say.

—Sarah Dessen, *The Truth About Forever*

The easiest people with whom to talk about your grief are those who have also lost someone. Those who have not want to comfort you and want to show that they care. Until you have been through loss, however, you are only guessing at what it is truly like.

Q: Do you find yourself having an indescribable bond between you and someone else who has lost a loved one? What can you do this week to connect with another person who is living the grieving life?

Year +

A dragonfly to remind me even though we are apart your spirit is always with me forever in my heart.

—Unknown

Some things remind us of the person who died, or send us a symbol of our loved one. This can be healing for some to think of the person each time we see this symbol, and it can give us a great feeling. Some common symbols are dragonflies, butterflies, birds (especially cardinals), hearts, horses, crosses, deer, a certain color … a lot of different things.

Q: Is there anything you resonate with that reminds you of your loved one? If so, is there something you can do with this—get a tattoo or make a quilt, car decal, keychain, shirt? If not, is there a reason why you do not want to associate something with the person who died?

Day 26

First Year

Nothing ever goes away until it teaches us what we need to know.

—Pema Chödrön

Take a moment, either in a journal or on a scrap of paper, to write down the most important thing you learned about yourself from the person you lost. You may have learned that you are more patient than you realized or stronger than you thought, that you love more deeply than you knew, or that you are loyal. Every person gives us a gift, and it is valuable to recognize each one as the precious treasure it is.

Q: What important thing(s) have you learned from the death of your person(s)?

Year +

It's easy to be forgetful when you're grieving, even forget those things that you believe most people wouldn't. –

—Liz Fichera, *You Are Here*

Don't hesitate to ask for help, even though some time has passed since your loss. Those who have lost someone know the truth—that the grief process is overwhelming for a period of time far longer than one would imagine.

Q: Do you have any guilt or reservations talking about your grieving journey now that time has passed? Have you ever felt that you "should" be farther along in your grief journey than you are? What steps can you take to give yourself some grace or permission to still have tough times?

Day 27

First Year

I still miss those I loved who are no longer with me but I find I am grateful for having loved them. The gratitude has finally conquered the loss.

—Rita Mae Brown

It can take a very long time to feel gratitude for the relationship you had. There is always a part of you that will long for one more hour together.

Q: How do you feel about the above quote? Put a label on those feelings, and sit with it a bit.

Year +

An important way to cope with grief is having an outlet, be it interpersonal, be it artistic, that will allow you to not have to contain your grief, but will give you an opportunity to express it, to externalize it to some degree.

—R. Benyamin Cirlin, grief counselor

Consider taking a class on a topic that interests you. It could be an academic subject, a skill, or a sport. Alternatively, join a new club, a book discussion group, or a political campaign. While you will most likely enjoy the experience of learning and being involved, one of the greatest benefits is that you will meet people who don't know you as someone who is grieving. It can become a place to connect with others without having to be reminded of your loss.

Q: What interests do you have that could lead to connections with other people?

Day 28

First Year

People think they know you. They think they know how you're handling a situation. But the truth is no one knows. No one knows what happens after you leave them, when you're lying in bed or sitting over your breakfast alone and all you want to do is cry or scream. They don't know what's going on inside your head—the mind-numbing cocktail of anger and sadness and guilt. This isn't their fault. They just don't know. And so they pretend and they say you're doing great when you're really not. And this makes everyone feel better. Everybody but you.

—William H. Woodwell Jr.

How many times have you responded "good" or "fine" when someone asks you how you are doing? If you were to be truthful, I'm guessing you might tongue-tie the person with your response.

Q: Is there something you can actually say that is more truthful? Think of some go-to responses for when you want to be truthful. An example might be "I'm having a tough day, but thank you for asking."

Year +

The caterpillar dies so the butterfly could be born. And, yet, the caterpillar lives in the butterfly and they are but one. So, when I die, it will be that I have been transformed from the caterpillar of earth to the butterfly of the universe.

—John Harricharan

Even though it is so hard to say goodbye to the people we love, they truly live on in those left behind. The skills they taught or the stories they told become your skills and your stories to pass along to someone else. Make the best parts of your loved one live on in you and those around you.

Q: What stories or memories of your loved one can you continue telling to pass along their wisdom, humor, and character?

Day 29

First Year

> When we lose someone we love, we must learn not to live without them, but to live with the love they left behind.
>
> —Unknown

The biggest question is How do you do that? Going through a death is not something a person usually is prepared for. You might also be navigating to help someone else grieve. That adds another layer of complication onto what you are already going through. If you are not careful, it may hinder your healing.

Q: What can you do just *for you to move forward and lean into the feelings?* Is there something you stop yourself from feeling—maybe crying because it is not an opportune time?

Year +

> Don't ever be ashamed of the scars life has left with you.
>
> —Unknown

A scar means the hurt is over and the wound is closed. It means you conquered the pain, learned a lesson, grew stronger, and moved forward. A scar is the tattoo of a triumph to be proud of. Don't allow your scars to hold you hostage. Don't allow them to make you live your life in fear.

> You can't make the scars in your life disappear, but you can change the way you see them. You can start seeing your scars as a sign of strength and not pain.
>
> —Life Learned Feelings

Q: What wounds in your life are you trying to heal? This could be things *besides* grief.

Day 30

First Year

It's oversimplified to say "Happiness is a choice."

—Lori Deschene

Happiness can take lots of choices; choices may be to accept ourselves as we are today, even if we are not perfect or completely whole at the moment. Happiness may be the choice to do things that are good for us, even if they are uncomfortable.

Q: Where do you go from here? What next steps are you going to take in your grief journey?

Year +

When someone you love becomes a memory, the memory becomes a treasure.

—Anonymous

Take a moment today to look at a photo, watch a home movie, or hold an object that reminds you of a special time with your loved one. Laugh, cry, and remember. Put that memory in a special place in your heart to treasure always.

Q: What can you do with another person who is grieving today? Maybe it is kids in your home—watch a favorite movie of the person who died. Or get out some photos. Maybe it is to call your sister and talk about a funny memory of your dad. Think beyond yourself today, and walk the grief journey with someone else for a few moments today.

Day 31

First Year

It occurred to me that grief is like a tunnel. You enter it without a choice because you must get to the other side. The darkness of it plays tricks on you and sometimes you can even forget where you are or what your purpose is. I believe that people, now and again, get lost or stuck in that tunnel …

—Loretta Nyhan, *Empire Girls*

Are you worried that you won't find your way out of the tunnel of grief? There is always a light to follow. With time and effort, you may work your way to find the other side. If you are struggling, you may need to seek out a support group, a counselor, or a trusted friend to help you see that light. The key right now is to know that you can absolutely find a way out.

Q: What do you keep running into over and over? Is it a typical emotion—fear, sadness, or guilt?

Year +

Gratitude for the present moment and the fullness of life now is the true prosperity.

—Eckhart Tolle

The attitude of gratitude is something that most people don't exercise very often. It's like working out; doing it once is not going to make much of a difference, but if it is routine, that's when you start to notice changes. November tends to be the month everyone talks about being grateful and being thankful, but what about the rest of the year or those bad or tough days?

Q: What can you do today to help flex your gratitude muscle every day? Set a reminder in your phone. Download a gratitude app. Buy a gratitude journal Put some time on your calendar to be intentional about gratitude or journaling. Make a gratitude jar, and put a slip of paper in it every day.

Day 32

First Year

Yet that grief and this joy were alike outside all the ordinary conditions of life; they were loop-holes, as it were, in that ordinary life through which there came glimpses of something sublime. And in the contemplation of this sublime something the soul was exalted to inconceivable heights of which it had before had no conception which reason lagged behind, unable to keep up with it.

—Leo Tolstoy, *Anna Karenina*

Grief and joy are the extremes of emotion. Although we think we seek joy, that is actually just a fleeting feeling. What you miss most right now is contentment, the feeling that all is calm and well. You may not be able to achieve that right now. Grief, the other extreme, is a forceful presence in your life. Although it may take a few weeks or months, contentment will return, and it will feel far sweeter for having been lost.

Q: Where are you right now on the emotional scale of grief and joy?

Year +

I'm thankful to have a family who takes eating as seriously as I do.

—Unknown

This quote made me laugh, and I realized how true it is. People find that once life moves on past the immediate reality of a death, it is easy to get wrapped up in everyday life again and not fully lean into grieving feelings or moments. As time passes, we see people return to laughing again and joking around with people the way they might have before a death. Some people start to realize all the good things they have in their life and how precious life actually is.

Q: Was there a point in your life when you felt the fog lift, and you started to feel a little bit as if life was back to a routine or that you could find some joy again? For some people it can be returning to work or school, even if they weren't ready. Some it's months or years after the death when they hit a realization. *What was the turning point in your life when you started to feel a little bit like you again? If you are not there yet, what do you think that will feel like?*

Day 33

First Year

I picture Cully tromping through that high, deep snow. That's how I feel physically from all of this. Moving through grief like it's a thick drift, exhausting but enlivening. It makes your muscles ache. It makes you feel you've inhabited your body completely.

−Kaui Hart Hemmings, *The Possibilities*

Grief can truly feel like an endless winter. In the actual season in colder climates, however, the sun will eventually melt the snow, and the beauty of spring will be revealed. Try to have hope today that the spring in your heart will come again as well.

Q: Is there a reminder you can give yourself that things can get better? A quote on your phone, a hope keychain, post-it note, or bracelet?

Year +

No one is going to stand up at your funeral and say, "She had a really expensive couch and great shoes." Don't make life about stuff.

−-Unknown

Think back to funerals you have attended, and think about any moments or stories that stand out in your mind. Most comments I get are how nice they looked, or how lovely the service was, or the funny stories people told—more about commemorating their life and the things they did or how they made you feel.

Q: How do you want your loved ones to remember you? Or what did you admire most about the person who died, and how can you live your life like them?

Day 34

First Year

> People grieve in different ways, some silently, some in anger, some in spite. Rarely does grief bring out the best in people, despite what local historians like to tell you.

> —Joanne Harris, *Five Quarters of the Orange*

You may miss the "real you," that person you were before you started to grieve. Don't worry; that person is still there. You can return to a more caring, compassionate version of yourself on the other end of the grief process.

Q: Do you see your grief as a journey, or are you looking at it trying to get to the end so you can move on?

Year +

> Just because someone carries it well doesn't mean it isn't heavy.

> —Unknown

Some people put on a tough exterior, either on purpose or by default in their nature. Knowing this, there is a "tough" person in your life that you can check on. Maybe ask them how they are doing—really. Or reach out to them to see if there is anything you can help them with. Extending kindness to those "tough" people might be that little bit that breaks the tough exterior.

Q: Have you been guilty of using the words "I'm fine" or "I'm good" when really you are not? Think through why this might be. So things don't get awkward if you *actually* say what is really going on? Or, is it because you don't want to share what is really going on? The next time you tell someone you are fine when really you are not, what can you do with those emotions? Maybe speaking a little bit of truth next time—"I'm having a tough day, but thank you for asking."

Day 35

First Year

There is greater clarity in the still waters of sadness, something not found in the babbling brooks of more sought after emotions.

—Shaun Hick

Feeling sad can be your new normal. That emotion has permeated every part of your life for weeks- such that you almost don't have to reflect and consider how you are feeling. The emotion is always sadness.

Take a break from sadness today. Put your face in the sun for ten minutes, or go for a walk in a local park. Take a step away from feeling down.

Q: What can you do today that you have not done in a long time?

Year +

I wasn't ready to say goodbye. I wasn't ready to let you leave me. I never would be. And every day, I am bleeding., but it was from you that I learned when life strikes me … I can bleed love and grace.

—Scribbles & Crumbs

Whoa, this one made me stop and think. Most people think they are pouring out sadness and bad emotions after a death. If you look at it a little differently and think of it as love actually coming out of you, now that is pretty cool.

Q: What did you love about the person who died? Make a list, or take a walk down memory lane. If it was a bad relationship, what good things came out of having this person in your life?

Day 36

First Year

Mostly it is loss which teaches us about the worth of things.

—Unknown

I always say that I didn't realize how precious life was until after my dad died unexpectedly. Then life got in the way, and I got busy with life. Then again I said it after my mom died unexpectedly. It is definitely a big realization for some people after a death: *that finality of a life*, that absence of them in your life. Some people dive deep into their faith, some dive deep into personal development, some dive deep into an adult beverage, some dive deep into gratitude. None of it is wrong; it is just the way some people choose to handle the deep unknown.

Q: Can you put a price on the thought of bringing your loved one back to life? For most there is no price. What are some things you value most in your life today? Is it things, time spent with people, experiences …?

Year +

We live and we die, but we are made of sterner stuff. The carbon atoms in our fingernails, the calcium in our bones, the iron atoms in our blood— all the countless trillions of atoms of which we are made—are ancient objects. They existed before us, before the Earth itself, in fact. And after each of us dies, they will depart from our bodies and do other things. Forever.

—Keith Heyer Meldahl,
Hard Road West: History and Geology along the Gold Rush Trail

Physical bodies are of this earth, but a person's spirit and memories can live on. Your loss can force you to face what you think happened to the essence or the spirit of your loved one. For some it is personal; for others it is a cultural belief or one of faith. This process is as much spiritual as it is emotional.

Q: What surprised you most about yourself after the loss?

Day 37

First Year

I think validation is one of the most beautiful gifts we can give the grieving.

—Angie Cartwright

When the opportunity arises, write a note, or take the time to call someone who has experienced a loss. Be a real listener when they want to talk, and be a shoulder to cry on. Providing comfort to someone else will help heal your heart as well. If you have an elderly neighbor you could always offer to give them a ride to the cemetery ….

Q: Who can you reach out to this week? Send a text, give them a call, send them a card, or flowers … flowers or the card can be anonymous if you don't want to reveal yourself.

Year +

Grief is a nasty game of feeling the weakest you have ever felt and morphing it into the strongest person you will have to become.

—Windgate Lane

This is my favorite new quote. It speaks volumes about the ups and downs of navigating through another's death. I walked my hardest walk of my life—down the aisle at church to see my father lying in a casket at the end of it. I broke down, wailed in the arms of my sister, but I made it to the casket. Since that day, I've told myself if I could do that, I could do anything. From there I had many ups and downs in life, but it built me up to be *much* stronger. I had the second hardest moment of my life when I had to walk into the hospital room six months pregnant to see my mom as "Jane Doe" puffed up and on a ventilator … and a few days later agreed to let her physical body go. After those moments in my life, I keep telling myself, "I got through that …."

Q: Can you see the worst and strongest parts of your life? Take time to reflect on the toughest moments or days of your life. *Then* take time to reflect on who you are today and what makes you a stronger person.

Day 38

First Year

> The sunlight now lay over the valley perfectly still. I went over to the graveyard beside the church and found them under the old cedars …. I am finding it a little hard to say that I felt them resting there, but I did. I felt their completeness as whatever they had been in the world.

> —Wendell Berry, *Jayber Crow*

Take a moment to go outside, or visualize in your mind a tall old tree. Look up into its branches. Start to think about what this tree has seen—the generations that have taken shelter under it from the sun, the children who have tried to climb it. Life rushes by, but this tree can symbolize for you generations of people who have been here, lived and loved, and moved on. Your loss is part of what this tree has seen, and like the new leaves in spring, you will eventually grow forward from this sorrow.

Q: How many generations of friends and family members has your loved one touched?

Year +

> You'll survive. That's the first thing they tell you after you lose someone. And you know what, they're right. In time, we all find a way to pick up the pieces and move on. What they forget to mention, however, is survival and happiness aren't always the same thing.

> —Beau Taplin

Whoa! Did you read that again? Would you consider yourself a happy person right now, today, as you sit here reading this? Most people say sure, they're happy, but are they really? Happiness is an inside job. You most likely cannot find it in other people, well except for laughing babies and cute puppies. They usually cheer people up. Besides those things, *you* are the only one who is responsible for your own happiness.

Q: Do you get through the day but barely, in survival mode? Or are you truly happy and grateful for your current life? Sometimes survival is okay; it gets you from point A to point B. Sometimes survival is all we can do to function and get through the day. But if it gets to the point where it is affecting your health, job, and relationships, please look into asking a professional for some guidance.

Day 39

First Year

But grief is the ultimate unrequited love. However hard and long we love someone who has died, they can never love us back. At least that is how it feels ….

—Rosamund Lupton, Sister

You will always love the person you lost. Grieving can feel lonely because you don't get to feel their love in return. You may want to write down what you would like to say to your loved one and what you think they would say back to you.

Q: Take time to ask them some questions. What do you think they would say back to you?

Year +

I have so much left to say to you.

—Unknown

Do you still carry on a conversation with the person who died? Some people call this "continuing bonds." It is the thought of having a relationship with the person even after they've died. We have heard many ideas behind this. People write a yearly letter to the person updating them on what happened this past year. Some write actual letters and keep them in a book. Other people talk to their loved one in the car. Some say they see signs of the person around; a bird, a dragonfly, a butterfly, an animal … Others might see a similar person walking down the street and react with a double take. Some say they visit them in dreams.

Q: In what ways can you try something new? Try any of the ideas above, or look up an idea of how you can continue the bond with the person who died.

Day 40

First Year

You were unsure which pain is worse—the shock of what happened or the ache for what never will.

—Unknown

Some sudden deaths or even some long-expected deaths can hit a person like a ton of bricks. *Then* the aftermath can set in, and people are shocked at what it is like. Really, there is nothing that can prepare you for a death and what it really is like until it happens. The reality of a life without that person can set in for some people.

Q: Have you dwelled on the continual loss of the person? They won't be at my wedding … I will never see their first day of kindergarten. … We won't trick or treat at their house again … Look back on the things you have gone through since the death, and be *proud* you made it through those "never wills." You made it to the other side. It may not have been pleasant, but you did it. If you are anticipating an upcoming holiday, what will you do to look for additional support?

Year +

I often used to say "I am fine, thank you," when people asked me how I was … their response would just be to say "great" and we all moved. What I longed for them to say was "I know you aren't fine, but one day you will be." To just know my pain was acknowledged and my aching heart was being heard would have meant the world. This is the gift we can all give to anyone who is walking the path of grief … listen to their whispers and breathe life into aching souls.

—Zoe Clark-Coates

I love this so much! Thinking through the actual pain you felt versus what you said when people asked how you were.

Q: Have you noticed anyone who has gone through a loss respond with "I'm good" … but you know they are not fine? What can you do next time you see this? Maybe you could send them a text that you would love to spend some time catching up with them soon, call them and ask if they want to talk, or send them some flowers saying you are thinking of them.

Day 41

First Year

But grief is a walk alone. Others can be there, and listen. But you will walk alone down your own path, at your own pace, with your sheared-off pain, your raw wounds, your denial, anger, and bitter loss. You'll come to your own peace, hopefully, but it will be on your own, in your own time.

—Cathy Lamb, *The First Day of the Rest of My Life*

Think of how you grew to care for or even love the person you lost. It was its own beautiful experience. Grieving is as unique as the love you shared with the special person you lost.

Q: What made your love unique for that person? Or what made your loss unique?

Year +

Anyone who has lost a loved one knows that you don't recover. Instead, you learn to incorporate their absence and memories into your life and channel your emotional energy towards others, and eventually, your grief will walk beside you instead of consuming you.

—Rashida Rowe

Whoa! I'm not sure if you are to this point or not, but that is a neat way to look at it: your grief will walk beside you and not consume you. Think back to when it consumed you. Maybe you couldn't function a full day without breaking down or living like a zombie, unable to comprehend what really happened.

I am super happy for you if you are past that and are able to get through the days in a more manageable way. Most understand that grief never will really go away—which is neat because that means there was some love there or connection to another soul that has changed you.

Q: When you think of grief, do you think of it as negative or positive? If your instinct is negative, what positives can you write down in the margins? (For instance, there was love there, you became more self-aware and compassionate ….)

Day 42

First Year

It takes a year, nephew … a full turn of the calendar, to get over losing someone.

—Annie Proulx, *The Shipping News*

It would be comforting to know exactly how long the grieving process takes. Everyone you talk to has their own advice, and books on the subject have differing opinions as well. The truth is that it is different for everyone.

Don't feel pressured by the calendar. Your grieving period will take as long as it takes, and you cannot actively control that. *Be good to yourself, and work through this time with a sense of patience rather than urgency.* Taking steps to lean into your feelings can help you work through grief in a healthier way.

Q: What have you heard about how long it takes to "get over" a loss? How would you feel if you were still struggling at that point in your life? Pretty crappy, right?! What can you do to remind yourself it takes time?

Year +

Isn't it funny how day by day nothing changes but when you look back everything is different.

—C. S. Lewis

I always like to go back to this quote. When you go through the motions to just get through the day, or to make it to the weekend, it can be tough to step back and see how much has changed.

Q: If you take a look back ten years, how much has your life changed with income, health, relationships? What about fifteen or twenty years?

Day 43

First Year

If he didn't love so deeply, he couldn't grieve so deeply. But he's drowning in it.

–Dee Henderson, *The Protector*

Think about how someone you know seemed when he or she was grieving. How did you feel being around that person? While it's tough to see yourself objectively, try to determine how you may be connecting with those around you. Think back to all the people who reached out or came to the funeral; a piece of that person's heart was reaching out to you, showing that they cared. On those tough days or moments try to remember all that love wrapped around you.

One of the kids' books I was just reading talked about how it is important to lean on family and friends in tough times. You don't have to face this alone. Yes, the grieving journey is yours to heal though, but leaning on those around you can help make it a bit easier.

Q: When was the last time you let someone help you? Make it a point to tell someone you are having a tough time with XYZ this week, or reach out to someone who said, "Let me know if you need anything." Letting someone help you can be a way to let some of the control go and lean into the care.

Year +

If there's even a slight chance at getting something that will make you happy, risk it. Life's too short, and happiness is too rare.

–A. R. Lucas

Think back to when you had extra free time, or back in college, high school, or middle school or even when you were a lot younger. Think through a list of things that you really enjoyed: music, kayaking, playing a sport, gardening, watching a show, going to a movie, reading, horseback riding, running, going to concerts, sleepovers with friends, bowling ….

Q: What are some things you used to enjoy doing that you haven't done in a long time? Make it a point to do one of those things this month. Put it in your calendar if you have to.

Day 44

First Year

> Grief … gives life a permanently provisional feeling. It doesn't seem worth starting anything. I can't settle down. I yawn, I fidget, I smoke too much. Up till this I always had too little time. Now there is nothing but time. Almost pure time, empty successiveness.

> —C. S. Lewis, *A Grief Observed*

You may be all over the place with emotions and what to do, or what not to do. Losing someone stinks!—to put it in a simple way. Nobody taught you how to deal with this. It is foreign for most people. Reach out to someone who has resources; try an online tailored program like Grief Your Way (www.griefyourway.com), an in-person grief group, a counseling center, your funeral home, or a church—all places that have many resources that can aid you in healing.

Some suggestions of things to help with time are to begin a project that is meaningful to you. You may want to label old photos or videos, donate clothing to a charity, or reorganize your bedroom. Take on a task that generates a tangible result, so that, upon its completion, you can look at it and see what you have achieved.

Q: What is the real reason you have not reached out for help? Is it a sense of guilt or fear of breaking down? Is it that talking out emotions sounds like too much to handle? If it's because you don't like sharing with strangers—dig deeper. Would you rather share with a friend, or just don't feel a connection with strangers to let them into your world?

Year +

May your choices reflect your hopes, not your fears.

—Nelson Mandela

Whoa! Most parents urge their children to make good choices, but what advice do you have for yourself on your choices in life?

Q: Are you hiding because of fear of failure, fear of looking foolish, fear of being too emotional, fear of speaking in front of people, fear of rejection? What if the choices you made all worked out in your favor or better? Try making a choice reflecting your hopes this week.

Day 45

First Year

I do hope that when the day comes, whether in 1, 10, or 100 years, I don't want you to think of me and feel sad.

−Esther Earl,
This Star Won't Go Out: The Life and Words of Esther Grace Earl

Do something special—be it lunch with a friend or a walk in the park with a relative—and take a photograph of it. You can start to build some new memories centered on what you are doing today.

Q: What would the person who died say about how you are doing mentally and physically if they were sitting right next to you today?

Year +

Self care is giving the world the best of you. Instead of what's left of you.

−Katie Reed

Many people think self-care is bubble baths and massages. By all means tell anyone you need to that is what you need to do. If you are functioning on "getting by," that also means others around you are getting the tired, exhausted, short-fused you. If you took time to wind down, de-stress, go fishing or hunting, read a book, or take a long overdue nap (put the phone away and stop scrolling social media) and worked on slowing down and being present—you might enjoy yourself a bit more, and those around you would get a better version of you as well.

Q: What does your self-care look like to you?

Day 46

First Year

We bereaved are not alone. We belong to the largest company in the world—the company of those who have known suffering.

—Helen Keller, *We Bereaved*

There will be times when you mourn the person you were before you experienced the loss of a loved one. Death can change a person.

Q: What deep down do you wish would have been different, either with the day they died, at the funeral, or shortly after? After you answer that question, ponder what really is at the root: do you have guilt for not being there, do you wish you had done something differently—is there remorse?

Year +

Be the things you loved most about the people who are gone.

—Unknown

This is another one of my favorite quotes. It is so stinking neat to think about. I loved my dad's humor and goofiness (and a ton of other things) and loved my mom's passion to help others and give back (among a ton of other things). I work to keep humor in my life, smile and laugh and bring humor to tough situations. I also have this strong pull to help others because I saw how much my mom loved giving back and how much of an impact that made on people and the community.

Q: What are all the things you loved about the people who are gone? (Write all over this page, or get out a new sheet of paper.) Take it a step further: what are all the things people love about you that they will miss when you are gone?

Day 47

First Year

> Take any emotion—love for a woman, or grief for a loved one, or what I'm going through, fear and pain from a deadly illness. If you hold back on the emotions—if you don't allow yourself to go all the way through them—you can never get to being detached, you're too busy being afraid. You're afraid of the pain, you're afraid of the grief. You're afraid of the vulnerability that loving entails.
>
> But by throwing yourself into these emotions, by allowing yourself to dive in, all the way, over your head even, you experience them fully and completely. You know what pain is. You know what love is. You know what grief is. And only then can you say, "All right. I have experienced that emotion. I recognize that emotion. Now I need to detach from that emotion for a moment."

—Mitch Albom, *Tuesdays with Morrie*

As you experience the grief process, try to have an awareness of how you are feeling and how those who share your pain are feeling. It helps to have self-awareness so that you can eventually use this time to grow and become a more thoughtful, empathetic person.

Q: What have you noticed since the death?

1. Do you cling to others to fill down time?
2. Do you shove emotions down so you don't cry in front of people? Do you have a drink to unwind and not deal with the sad feelings?
3. Do you look forward to time with family and friends?
4. Do you seek out ways to help others?
5. Do you find yourself looking for grief groups, books, or resources?

If you said yes to number 1 or 2, maybe there is something you can do this week to take a baby step in a healthy and healing direction.

If you answered yes to any of the last three, it sounds like you are taking positive steps.

Year +

> Tears have always been easier to shed than explain.

> —Marty Rubin

Sometimes it feels like there are no words to accurately describe what grief feels like. As with any pain, you can't remember it with precision after the fact, which can be a blessing.

Q: What metaphors do you use to describe grief? Roller coaster, waves of the ocean, strings being cut and repaired, a ripped heart ….

Day 48

First Year

Books give me an escape from reality, even if it's only for a few minutes.

—Just Keep Smiling

I've always been a person who felt like I needed to learn more or hear another side of a story to look at it from all angles. I love to read nonfiction books about people's lives or books and articles about what they learned throughout life that made them better people. But every once in a great while I turn to a funny fiction book or book on CD to listen to in the car. I've noticed that I smile more, goof around a bit more, and overall feel happier.

Q: Is there anything you enjoy doing that you don't often do that lifts your mood up a bit? Or think about something that remains the same all the time—the music you listen to, the TV you watch, the things you read ....

Year +

Time passes but not one day goes by that you are not here in my heart. The day you died was not just a date on a calendar, it was the day when my very existence changed forever.

—Unknown

It wasn't a moment in time but a date and life after. Sometimes people say they look at life as the before and after the death. There is a quote called "The Dash" that is pretty neat. Take time to look it up online, or ask someone if they have heard of it. I talked about this at my mother's funeral. It's a powerful thought. On a headstone you see the date the person is born and the date they died. In the middle is the dash.

Q: What do you want people to remember about you during your "dash"—the middle part between your birthdate and death date? What legacy do you want to leave behind?

Day 49

First Year

Here's what I know: death abducts the dying, but grief steals from those left behind.

—Katherine Owen, *Seeing Julia*

When you have experienced a loss, you can feel like a victim. Something precious was taken away from you, and there is a definite helplessness to that. You *can* make the active decision to not be a victim of your grief. Feel the sadness, but work through the pain proactively each day to take back the control.

Q: How do you do that? – Sounds great, but really *what can you do?* Journaling, punching a pillow/ kickboxing, ax throwing, hitting some balls (golf, baseball, or soccer), screaming into a pillow, taking time to cry, talking to others about what you are going through, setting up a counseling appointment, reaching out to a doctor or chaplain or grief support, watching movies that make you cry, singing super loud and letting the tears come out, playing music to get your feelings out …. *How are you going to lean into your feelings right now?*

Year +

I'm still grieving, I'm still upset. And that's okay.

—Unknown

You do you … every person is different, every relationship is different, every death is different, every person's response and grieving journey is different. Maybe you feel you are in a good spot, or maybe you feel stuck and don't know which way to turn.

You are on a journey, and nobody is going to go through a death the same way you do—but that also means you are in charge of taking steps to move forward in your grief journey.

Q: Fill in the blank: I'm still _____ and that's okay. This month I plan to _____ to help lean into my feelings.

Day 50

First Year

Life Lesson 3: You can't rush grief. It has its own timetable. All you can do is make sure there are lots of soft places around – beds, pillows, arms, laps.

—Patti Davis, *Two Cats and the Woman They Own:*
or Lessons I Learned from My Cats

Show yourself the same patience that you show to everyone else in your life. The key is to believe that you will heal from this. You will be changed, but you will heal nonetheless.

Q: What thing in your life are you being hard on yourself for? What things in your life do you put your own high standards or expectations on? What in your life do you make harder for yourself? What in your life can you put on pause or get help with for a little while?

Year +

Grief lasts longer than sympathy, which is one of the tragedies of the grieving.

—Elizabeth McCracken

You probably haven't received a sympathy card in quite a while. Most of your friends, family, neighbors, and coworkers know about your loss and have already reached out to you. You may be feeling fairly isolated and forgotten.

While you can't force people to reach out to you again, it can be helpful to reach out to someone else who needs you. Offer to run an errand for a busy parent, pick up groceries for an elderly neighbor, or send a card to someone who could use the pick-me-up that comes from being remembered. The process of acting to help another person will make you feel more alive and connected.

After people stopped saying, "I'm sorry for your loss," it seemed like the world moved on, but I didn't, and I felt offended that nobody had sympathy anymore. It can be an odd feeling of wanting that sympathy, but not wanting attention on you. It might hurt when the world moves on and doesn't acknowledge your super huge pain.

Q: What else are you grieving about? There is a phenomenon called "secondary loss." Beyond the surface of the death of your loved one, what else are you grieving the loss of? A childhood home, the role of being a parent, the role of caregiver, the loss of a second income, the loss of seeing a child grow up .... It can be important to take a step back and see that you really are going through a lot more than it might seem, but know that you can get through it in a healthy way, and there can be hope for happier times.

Day 51

First Year

I used to think grief was a feeling and something you purely dealt with in your mind, oh how wrong I was! It is a process that involves your heart, mind, body and soul. Every part of you grieves, every cell weeps. If we use our energy to fight experiencing it we have less strength available to us to bravely face it. So lay down your sword and take off your armour. Just feel it, let it take hold, and then the walk of healing will be gifted to you.

–Zoe Clark-Coates

Some people avoid talking about the person who died. Others change the channel when a sad commercial comes on to avoid tears. People even change the radio station when a triggering song comes on to avoid those feelings. It is human nature to shield ourselves from sadness or intense emotions.

Q: Honestly, what have you been avoiding?

Year+

One of the most challenging things I've had to learn is that healing must be intentional. There is no one golden day that comes and saves you from all your misery. Healing is a practice. You have to decide that it's what you want to do and actively do it. You have to make a habit out of it. Once I learned that, I only looked back to see how far I came.

–The Minds Journal

This goes back to the saying that you are in charge of your life. Are you sitting around waiting for someone to rescue you from your life? The only way to make a change is to make a choice.

Q: What can you do this week to do something for you in your grief journey?

Day 52

First Year

Courage doesn't always roar. Sometimes courage is the little voice at the end of the day that says I'll try again tomorrow.

—Mary Anne Radmacher

You may have had several days, even weeks, where you felt like you were doing a little better ... not great, but a little better. Then it hit again like a ton of bricks. Grief sometimes plays cruel tricks where you think you're handling it, and then you have a setback. This process is long and grueling. Be patient with yourself, and remember that tomorrow is another day.

Q: Think through your recent peaks and valleys. What is one valley that stands out to you? What response or reaction did you have to that valley? How you react to the small things might be how you react to the big things.

Year +

She was always fighting a battle, but her smile would never tell you so.

—Nikki Rowe

Sometimes the strongest people carry grief inside and never let anyone know what is really going on inside. If this is you, know that you are not alone. If you know someone who is strong who lost a person, reach out to them. One of my sisters was having a tough week, I could tell, but she is not one to really "spill the beans" about what is going on. I decided to send her an edible arrangement from no sender .... She said it lifted her mood instantly. (Eventually she did figure out it was from me.) It's nice to receive something out of the blue as a reminder from the world that you are not alone and people care.

Q: What can you do this week to let your guard down a bit? Reach out to someone who is strong-willed to let them know you are there for them. Or send someone who rarely shares feelings an anonymous gift of something that would show someone cares.

Day 53

First Year

Grief can't be shared. Everyone carries it alone, his own burden, his own way.

−Anne Morrow Lindbergh

It can be surprising, even shocking, that others who had a relationship with the person you lost are grieving so differently. The fact that they are crying more than you, talking less, seem so content, or any other difference is hard to understand.

The grieving process is hugely different among us all, even when we are working through the loss of the same person. One way is not better or worse than another … it is simply different. At times, trying to talk with someone whose process does not match your own might not be helpful. Instead, you may want to turn to someone who understands and appreciates your grieving process.

Q: Is there anyone in your life who has gone through a similar loss that you could reach out to? Or is there a virtual or in-person grief group you could attend?

Year +

You're not stuck. You're just committed to certain patterns of behavior because they helped you in the past. Now those behaviors have become more harmful than helpful. The reason why you can't move forward is because you keep applying an old formula to a new level in your life. Change the formula to get a different result.

−Unknown

Whoa! History repeats itself. If you aren't learning from your situations and problems, they will come back around. Man oh man, read that quote again … or two more times.

Q: What was your last big problem, and what was the root lesson you should have learned?

Day 54

First Year

Change the way you look at things and the things you look at change.

—Wayne W. Dyer

Take out a concrete object today that reminds you of your loved one. It could be a photograph, a letter, or something that belonged to that person. Even if the object initially makes you feel sad, think of at least two things about it that make you feel happy. It is not an easy assignment, and you may not be able to do it yet. Keep trying, though, as it will help you move past your grief into a place of greater contentment.

Q: What two things can you do today or this week that initially make you feel sad? Remember, if you can't get to the point where you find two things that make you happy, it's okay. This may take time.

Year +

You can't heal if you keep pretending you're not hurt.

—Unknown

Strong-willed people tend to shelter their feelings. The only way you will move forward in your grieving journey is taking it into your own hands. This might seem obvious by now, but as the years go on, it is harder to see that you might be sheltering feelings and grief.

(if you are the opposite, how do you think harnessing your emotions through writing, or another way might help?)

Q: What do you typically do to hide your feelings?

Day 55

First Year

> We all make mistakes, have struggles, and even regret things in our past. But you are not your mistakes, you are not your struggles, and you are here *now* with the power to shape your day and future.

> —Steve Maraboli, *Unapologetically You: Reflections on Life and the Human Experience*

You decide today who you are going to be and what you are going to do. The control you have over yourself and your actions is actually an important part of your healing. Your loved one being gone makes you feel like you have no control. However, you do control a lot of the pieces of your life. Having an awareness of that may help you feel less like a victim of your loss.

Q: What do you see in your grief that is out of your control? Emotions, situations … Think through what you *can* control … how you react, your attitude ….

Year +

> Your current situation is giving you an opportunity to re-evaluate what you want.

> —Tashabee

People don't often take a step back from life and assess what is really going on. Whatever is going on in your life can be looked at through many lenses.

Q: What would a wise old person (a grandma, old teacher) tell you about your current situation?

Day 56

First Year

To live in hearts we leave behind is not to die.

−Thomas Campbell

Write down one thing today that you learned from the person you lost. Put it in your pocket, and take it out whenever you feel you need to get through the day. Perhaps tomorrow you will not need the concrete reminder of the legacy left by such a special person in your heart.

Q: What can you carry around with you today or this week as a reminder?

Year +

I waited for dawn, but only because I had forgotten how hard mornings were. For a second I'd be normal. Then came the dim awareness of something off, out of place. Then the truth came crashing down and that was it for the rest of the day. Sunlight was reproof. Shouldn't I feel better than I had in the dead of night.

−Francine Prose, *Goldengrove*

When you least expect it, there will be a morning when you wake up and forget about your loss. Try not to feel guilty, for it is a sign of progress. While it may not happen again for a long time, waking up without sadness will eventually be the norm.

Q: Have you felt guilty about anything in relation to the death? Is there anything about the guilt that you can work past, or can you see any meaning behind it?

Day 57

First Year

What a beautiful thing it is to be able to stand tall and say, "I fell apart, and I survived."

—Daily Quotes

Many people are going through something: grief, loss, or another life-altering situation. It is easy to forget that we aren't the only ones in the world going through some tough stuff. You made it through the day of the death; you made it through the day of the funeral and burial; you made it through the next few days. You survived the worst days so far. Be proud of that!

Q: What are you most proud of?

Year +

There are some who bring a light so great to the world that even after they have gone the light remains.

—Love Lives On

That is so true of so many people who have died. Man, I think back to the people who showed up to my parents' funerals—so many people. I had no idea who half of the people were. It was amazing to see how many lives they touched. I always think back to the volunteer work my mom did and the lives she touched, and with my dad being a teacher, the kids he helped or encouraged. It always inspires me to be better in this world.

Q: What do you envy most about the person who died?

Day 58

First Year

What happens when you let go, when your strength leaves you and you sink into darkness, when there's nothing that you or anyone else can do, no matter how desperate you are, no matter how you try? Perhaps it's then, when you have neither pride nor power, that you are saved, brought to an unimaginably great reward.

—Mark Halperin

Can you let go of your grief for one day? You may not be ready quite yet. Try to involve yourself in a project or hobby today that frees your mind, even if it's only for a short time.

Q: What have you done lately to free your mind or give your mind a break?

Year +

If people knew how much I truly missed you, they would wonder how I am still breathing.

—Sandra Melloul, Heavensbook Angels

Man oh man, love can run so deep. If you haven't been through the death of someone close, you won't know what it is like. It is the toughest thing many people go through, and the toughest journey people navigate after a death. Just today a lady told me if you haven't gone through a loss, you will never really understand. In my head I was thinking, *Spot on!*

Q: How would you describe life after death to someone in simple terms (or think of how you would describe it to a child)?

Day 60

First Year

If you suppress grief too much, it can well redouble.

—Molière

You do not have to pretend to be the strong person that your family, friends, or even society assumes that you are. You may not want to cry, but you may want to find an outlet for the intense emotions that come with grief. If the tears won't come, you should do something physical to release some of that pressure. Taking a walk, running, or riding a bike can be helpful ways to handle the daunting feelings of grief.

Q: Think back to a time when you were laughing so hard that you had tears in your eyes, and it wouldn't stop, or a time when your emotions were over the top. Can you see how that might be suppressed emotions coming out? What is your go-to "emotional release"?

Year +

"Grief sucks." -Said Everyone Ever.

—What's Your Grief

This is my new favorite quote ... and 100 percent true. It is not fun. It is not easy. It can be lonely. There is no one to show you a road map of how to make it better. It stinks—but obviously you know this firsthand.

Q: How would you end this sentence? "Grief _____."

Day 61

First Year

Thinking and talking about death need not be morbid; they may be quite the opposite. Ignorance and fear of death overshadow life, while knowing and accepting death erases this shadow.

—Lily Pincus

It is important that you find someone in your life that has also lost someone close to them. It may be a family member, but it could also be someone that you connect with online or as part of a support group. You may not need to talk about your loss every day, but there will be days when you need to have someone to whom you can just say, "Today is tough," knowing that the person on the phone or reading your email understands. Having that moment where you feel safe and understood is important. If you haven't found someone to fill that role, you should begin trying to do so. It will make those flashes of pain much easier to bear.

Q: Do you have someone you can turn to? How would you rank their level of support on a scale from 1 to 10? If you do not have someone, or their level of support is low, consider reaching out for resources or groups in your community.

Year +

Strength is what we gain from the madness we survive.

—Unknown

You are strong because of what you have gone through in life. Please don't think any differently. We all struggle at some point in our lives and especially after the death of someone. It can knock us down—hard! But your battle scars show you stood up when you got knocked down. Maybe you are only halfway up, but you were strong enough to start standing. Be proud of that.

People often comment, "Oh, you are so strong," when a person goes through a tough death. People mean well, but most of us are put in a situation where we just have to be strong; there's no other choice. Life keeps moving, and responsibilities are still there.

Q: What events in your life have made you a stronger or more compassionate person?

Day 62

First Year

Death ends a life, not a relationship.

—Jack Lemmon

What defines a relationship? Many would argue that a relationship is the bond you have with another person. That bond, of course, varies a lot depending upon the person with whom you share it. However, the connection that you have is one that is everlasting and most certainly transcends death.

When your partner passes on, the relationship still remains. You don't have to use the past tense when you think about your loved one. Say to yourself, "I love this person," rather than "I loved this person." It is a small change but one that might help your heart know that you don't have to abandon that relationship but see it as an important part of your life today.

Q: What phrase do you catch yourself saying or correcting? "I was married", "my husband … late husband", "I have three kids … I have two and one died." How does it feel correcting those statements to keep it in the present instead of past tense? You *are* still a wife. You *do* still have three kids. An action item for this month is to practice keeping that bond and relationship alive with the person who died and still see them as everlasting, even if you cannot see them

Year +

My story is filled with broken pieces, terrible choices and ugly truths. It's also filled with a major comeback, peace in my soul and a grace that saved my life.

—Sunday Morning With Sandy

Broken crayons still color, my friend. A piece of you is broken, but that doesn't mean you can't still move forward and heal. The word *broken* means not functioning properly or torn and fractured (dictionary. com). That sounds about right when you think about the moments after you found out a person died. For some it might have been a relief, but how did your heart feel when they were not on this earth anymore?

Q: How would you describe what it felt like when you heard your person died?

Day 63

First Year

Unfortunately, there is no expiration date on grief.

—Elizabeth Czukas

Grief is something that lives with us for the rest of our lives. The pain can dissipate as time passes on, though. You are now in a club that nobody ever wants to be in, *the grief club.* We all went through a tough death and will live with that for the rest of our lives. The good news is that you can go at your own pace.

Q: How do you really *feel about where you are today in your grief journey?*

Year +

What you want to show yourself is that you can control the direction of your thoughts.

—Abraham Hicks

Your feelings determine your reality. Read that one again: your feelings determine your reality. Powerful stuff, friends! I've talked about this in the past, how two people can watch a story and have very different perspectives on whether it is frightening or beautiful. Are you looking through the lens of darkness or light?

Q: Think back at what negative thoughts or comments you have said today (or this week). How would you rephrase them to have a positive spin?

Day 64

First Year

Accepting death doesn't mean you won't be devastated when someone you love dies. It means you will be able to focus on your grief, unburdened by bigger existential questions like, "Why do people die?" and "Why is this happening to me?" Death isn't happening to you. Death is happening to us all.

—Caitlin Doughty

You are not alone in your journey even though it might feel like it right now. The reality is that a large number of people in your town have experienced a loss as well. About 2.5 million people die in the United States annually, each leaving an average of five grieving people behind. That's a lot!

Q: Do you think you are at the point where you have accepted the death of your person? Do you still feel alone in your journey?

Year +

You are strong enough to handle whatever's coming, even if it doesn't feel like it right now.

—Tiny Buddha

Does that sound realistic to you, or like a quote that is blowing smoke? You were strong enough to get through the day your person died; you are strong enough to be here today. I always said if I could walk down that aisle at the church to see my dad dead in a casket when I was twenty-two, I could do anything. That thought has got me through a lot of tough stuff in my life.

Q: What tough things have you seen people close in your life get through? (Think about reaching out to them and telling them how proud you are of them for going through it. You might be surprised to hear what they say.)

Day 65

First Year

I aspire to be the widow my husband would be proud of … still.

−Mary Lee Robinson

I love this quote. It is an interesting way of thinking about making something good out of a terrible experience. Think of the person who died. If they were sitting next to you right now, would they be proud of how you conduct yourself or sad to see you are having a tough time functioning?

Q: What can you do today to take a step in a possible direction to make your loved one proud of you?

Year +

Imagine this: If you had $86,400 in your account and someone stole $10 from you, would you be upset and throw all of the remaining $86,390 away in hopes of getting back at the person who took your $10? Or move on and live? Right, move on and live. See, we have 86,400 seconds each day. Don't let someone's negative 10 seconds ruin the remaining 86,390. Don't sweat the small stuff, life is bigger than that.

−Tiny Buddha

Whoa! That is super powerful to think about. For me, I'm my own worst enemy; that person who took $10 or more is usually myself. I tend to be hard on myself and have a lot of negative talk at times. I need to remind myself that it's just a negative way to look at something, and the rest of my day does not need to throw away the rest of the money. This makes me think of the quote, "It's a bad day, not a bad life." Sometimes we can get into a funk and don't realize we are letting it consume our day, our week, or even our year—yes, I'm quoting the show Friends here.

Q: Can you think back to someone (or maybe yourself) who triggered you to throw away the remaining $86,390?

Day 66

First Year

Grief is a powerful source of information about who we are, when we dare to look.

—Antonio Sausys

This one really made me think. How has grief caused you to act or react in certain ways? Were you angry at others for no reason or maybe had problems crying after the death? Did you turn to a cocktail when you were stressed or didn't want to deal with what was going on inside? Did you shut others out or really cling to someone? All rhetorical questions, but take some time to think about who you are as a result of your grief.

Q: How would you describe your reactions, actions, inactions, and interactions after the death?

Year +

It had been many months since I'd shed tears for Tomaso, but grief is like that. It's not a continuous process; it comes in waves. You can keep it at bay for a time, like a dam holding back a lake, but then something triggers an explosion inside of you, shattering the wall and letting loose a flood.

—Paul Adam, *Paganini's Ghost*

We tend to call these "grief triggers." They usually come out of the blue and can be intense emotionally. I was the girl sobbing in a Kohl's department store in the clothing section one day, because of a song that came on overhead—and this was four years after my mom died. They can come on at any time. But as you do the healing work, they usually are farther and farther apart.

I went to the chiropractor today, and randomly "The Ring of Fire" by Johnny Cash came on. Yes, it was one of my dad's favorite songs—and yes, I have heard it hundreds of times since he died—but for some reason today it made me get all teary-eyed. (And I'm not a big crier.)

Q: Thinking back, have you had any of these "grief triggers" in the past? What did you do with them— hold it in or let it out?

Day 67

First Year

One of the grubby truths about a loss is that you don't just mourn the dead person, you mourn the person you got to be when the lost one was alive. This loss might even be what affects you the most.

—Meghan O'Rourke, *The Long Goodbye*

You can grieve your person and you can grieve the life you used to have; that is a real thing! You can grieve the life you had planned with the person who died. Grief is complicated. You can also be going through grief in relation to relationships and tangible things. If you want to look more into this, look up the term "secondary grief."

Q: What are you grieving besides the person who died?

Year +

When someone you love dies, you get a big bowl of sadness put down in front of you, steaming hot. You can start eating now, or you can let it cool and eat it bit by bit later on. Either way, you end up eating the whole thing. There's really no way around it.

—Ralph Fletcher, *Fig Pudding*

Such a good analogy around grief! Some people push the bowl aside and don't touch it for weeks, months, or even years. When they finally get back around to that bowl, it has a lot of yuck on it, and it's worse to eat. The more you push that bowl away, the worse it will be to eat later on. Working through your grief now can help you process it in a healthier way.

Don't feel like you need to do all the work now and get through that bowl as fast as you can. Life will fill it back up if you aren't taking care of yourself. If you need a break from grief work, take a break. Taking care of your mind, body, and soul is also healing work.

Q: Do you feel your mind, body, and soul are in balance today? If not, what seems out of sorts that you might need some extra care on?

Day 68

First Year

We identify ourselves through the persons and things we are attached to; when we lose them, we lose part of who we are.

—Antonio Sausys

Did you lose an identity when the person died? Maybe you lost something like a sense of companionship, or your kids' father figure, the title *wife* or *son*. There are so many layers to death.

Q: What part of you also died with your loved one?

Year +

Don't be discouraged because things aren't happening as fast as you'd like. All seasons serve a purpose.

—Live Oola

Some people might not agree with this quote. If you don't, I'd encourage you to think about why and the reason behind it. (I'm not saying it's wrong not to agree with the statement.) What I have found for people who do not agree is that it's because they feel they are a victim in their current season.

Think through some tough times in your life from the past, and write out or talk to another person about what positive thing came out of that tough experience.

Q: What positive things came out of some tough times in your life?

Day 69

First Year

Among other things, Kathryn knew, grief was physically exhausting.

—Anita Shreve, *The Pilot's Wife*

Physical symptoms of grief are a real thing! Feeling drained, or having unusual aches and pains, forgetfulness, digestive issues, increased trips to the bathroom, headaches or migraines—these physical symptoms (and more) can be related to your grief. (Please consult your doctor if you are having any major problems.) A lot of people report having trouble sleeping as well.

Q: Do you suffer from any physical symptoms of grief? Have you seen other grievers who have complained of any of these symptoms? Please consult your physician if any symptoms are too much and affect your daily life or work.

Year +

The highest tribute to the dead is not grief, but gratitude.

—Thornton Wilder

This one is a challenge to you- get out a piece of paper, your phone, talk-to-text, computer … anything to actually write this out.

Q: What 25 things are you grateful for when you think about your life or the person who died? If you are ready to *really* stretch yourself, write 25 more. (Could be traits they had, wisdom they gave you, lessons you learned, times you spent together ….)

Day 70

First Year

I had met death before, in different forms—I knew quite well the pattern of my grieving. First came shock, and then tears, and then a bitter anger, followed by a softer grief that time would wear away.

—Susanna Kearsley, *The Splendour Falls*

Nobody really tells you that your grief journey will be filled with all kinds of emotions all over the place. You are not broken—well, your heart might be, but you as a person are a body with a lot of new, intense emotions you may not have dealt with before. People usually don't read a book or learn what it's like to grieve *before* a death happens. And even if you do, as in the case of an expected death, it still never really prepares you for what your life is actually like in the *after*.

Q: What have been some things that came up that you weren't prepared for after the death of your person?

Year +

Don't try to silence your grief … if you do, what started as a purr can quickly become a roar.

—Zoe Clark-Coates

I'm tough. I don't cry. Feelings are dumb. Nobody is going to tell me how to go through steps of grief, since they haven't lived my life. Those are all things I thought after my dad died. So I pushed grief to the wayside and didn't deal with it. Well, that came back to bite me in many ways. It wasn't until five years later when my mom died that I realized I was shoving it all down. I wouldn't even watch a movie that I thought might be sad because I didn't want to cry. Some people develop bad coping strategies by doing this; some push off the healing journey for years or even decades. I've heard people say their loved one has been gone twenty or thirty years, and they just now realize they haven't really dealt with the death yet. It's okay; you can take a step at any time.

Q: Do you honestly think you have been taking steps to work through the death? If not, why?

Day 71

First Year

Funerals seem less about comforting the souls of these dearly departed than about comforting the people they leave behind.

—Rin Chupeco

Think back to the funeral, memorial service, celebration of life, burial, or any commemoration you may have had to celebrate their life. Was there a lot of support and comfort for your family? Did anyone send flowers or plant a tree in memory of your loved one, send a card, text, or call? That is support, that is community—that is love! Think of all those people who took time to go to a store, send a card, or call ….

Q: Who has been your biggest supporter or rock through all of this? Consider sending them a thank-you text, note, or card.

Year +

If they wanted nothing more than for you to be happy in life … Why would that change, in death?

—John Polo

Whoa! Did your person always wish for you to have a good life and be happy? Maybe in honor of them you can strive to do that! Easier said than done, of course. If you take inventory of your life, how would you rate yourself on a scale of 1 to 10, 10 being amazing, for the following categories:

1. Health _____
2. Relationships _____
3. Finances _____
4. Mind _____
5. Activity level _____

6. Stressless _____
7. Sleep _____
8. Diet _____
9. Coping with emotions _____

Q: Circle the one that you think needs the most improvement. Then put a star next to the one that you are doing a great job at! Underline one in the middle. *Do you think you could work on the one in the middle? Try to get a 10 percent improvement from now to next month.*

Day 72

First Year

Never compare your grief. You—and only you—walk your path.

—Nathalie Himmelrich, *Grieving Parents: Surviving Loss as a Couple*

You and another person will go through completely different grief journeys. Even if you lost the same person (a sister, say, or a dad), each person's grief is complex. It all depends on your relationship with that person, how you handle stress, how you take care of yourself, what you do in tough times—so many facets make up this complicated ball called grief.

What I can say is that by taking care of yourself and walking your *own* grief journey, you can help others heal as well. Another person might see how you are improving your mood or appearance, and it could trigger them to take action in their own grief journey.

On the flip side, if you feel as if you are not as far along in the healing process as someone else, that is playing the comparison game. You might not know what is going on inside that person or how much work they did to get to where they are now.

Q: Take a moment to do an inventory of your life: how do you think you are doing honestly *right now?*

Year +

Grief from a parent's death feels like you want to go home but can't ever again.

—AEM Writing Grief

Your home, your security, your safe place is gone! That is true with a lot of different types of death. After I lost my dad, things never felt the same, almost as if my innocence was gone. Home was not the same. Then after my mom died, it literally was gone: we sold my parents' house. That "home" feeling isn't something I have anymore, and that is sad!

Q: What do you feel you lost besides your person?

Day 73

First Year

I told someone "welcome to the grief club" and I'm sure I sounded crazy. For clarity … We're not here by choice. Nobody wants to be here. Yet somehow I'm bonded with people I've never met over this pain of my grief. They get it. I get it. You get it. Once you're in. … sadly you just get it. So, welcome to the grief club.

—Glitter and Grief

You get it, I get it … it's a sad phrase, but oh so true! Do you know other people who belong to this club? There are different chapters. Spouse loss, child loss, suicided loss … you get the idea. But we are all tied to the same topic of a friend or family member who died.

Q: Who can you reach out to today who is in the club to ask how they are really *doing or plan a coffee date just to spend time with them?*

Year +

Grief club (n) – the club nobody asked to join, where membership is automatic after losing someone you love.

—Glitter and Grief

I hate to say it, but welcome to the club. We never want new members, but it happens every day. We are glad to comfort you and be here for you! If you haven't gone through a tough death, you have no idea what it is like. That is the honest truth! Nobody can prepare you for what it will be like. Sure, there are ways to learn what emotions might come, but until you are in the middle of it, you'll never understand.

Q: What is one thing you wish someone had told you about life after their death?

Day 74

First Year

What you choose to focus on … will grow.

—Unknown

Is your brain a positive one or a negative one? If you had to tip the scales one way or the other, would you say a day in your head is more positive or negative? That answer probably is also mirrored in your life. If your mind is tipped more to negative thoughts, are there a lot of things going wrong in your life these days? If your mind is tipped more to the positive, are unexpected things happening in your life that are good?

Q: What can you do today to make your mind 10 percent more positive today? Watch a funny show, funny videos, do something that makes your heart happy, look at some photos, do some positive affirmations … spend time with people you love.

Year +

No matter what the issue is, don't try to justify why you don't feel good. And don't try to justify why you should feel differently. Don't try to blame whatever it is you think the reason is that's keeping you from feeling good. All of that is wasted effort. Just try to feel better right now.

—Abraham-Hicks

Think about your right now—today, as you are reading this. What are you feeling? Stop with the "shoulding" and blame. What do you want to be feeling right now?

Q: What do you think is blocking you from feeling true happiness? Is it a story you keep telling yourself or a label of shame or guilt hanging over you?

Day 75

First Year

It took an instant to lose you, and it will take my entire *lifetime* to grieve the loss of you. *Grief* never ends because *love* never ends. I will love you, and ache for you until my very last breath.

—Angela Miller

Life changes in a second. You know this, I know this. Your life is not the same anymore. Most people talk about the before and after. The reality is your life is now in the after; it could be days after, weeks after, or many, many years after.

Q: If your person were here today and you got one hour with them, what would you do?

Year +

Missing my child is not me living in the past. It's me loving my child in the present.

—Angela Miller

That is a powerful quote! Read that again. It is just a different relationship with that person now. Their physical body is not on earth, but they are still your child, dad, mom, grandma, aunt, or friend. That relationship is still yours to keep. People often call this "continuing bonds."

Q: How do you respond when someone you don't know asks about the person who died? (Example: the checkout lady asks, "What are you doing with your mom this Mother's Day?")

Day 76

First Year

Growth is painful. Change is painful. But nothing is as painful as staying stuck somewhere you don't belong.

—Curate Well Co.

Maybe you have outgrown the stage of life you are in. Are you stuck here because change is tough and painful? Are you stuck because you don't want to dig into those tough feelings? Take an inventory of your life.

Q: Finish the sentence: I don't make a change because change is _____.

Year +

Grief is never something you get over. You don't wake up one morning and say, "I've conquered that; now I'm moving on." It's something that walks beside you every day. And if you can learn how to manage it and honor the person that you miss, you can take something that is incredibly sad and have some form of positivity.

—Terri Irwin

That is such a neat and comforting quote to me. I hope to strive to be at peace and be able to find comfort and positivity in the death of my parents. I think everyone hopes to be there someday.

Some people get there, and some people never get there. Every grief journey is different. Every person's level of trauma is different; every person's healing journey is different.

Q: Think back … what are the top two or three things that have helped you find comfort in tough times?

Day 77

First Year

> Keep going. No matter how bad things are right now. No matter how stuck you feel. No matter how many days you've spent crying. No matter how many days you've spent wishing things were different. No matter how hopeless and depressed you feel. I promise you won't feel this way forever. Keep going.
>
> —Unknown

It can be hard to believe that statement if you are feeling stuck or exhausted living in your current state. It is possible to keep going and feel better. Maybe it is time to try something new. Google counselors in your area, or join a grief group; start journaling or talking to friends about how you *really* are doing. People don't know what they don't know. Nobody knows your inner thoughts or feelings, and most likely people are not going to try to pull them out of you. It is your job to express what is going on.

Q: What do you really *need right now?*

Year +

> Feelings are just visitors, let them come and go.
>
> —Mooji

Maybe you are like me and always stuffed sadness and tears down because that is what you did as a child. It can be hard to let the feelings come and go without resistance, just in life but especially in your grief. Our bodies resist these emotions because they are tough, and our brain wants to protect us from the hurt. Understanding and exploring your patterns with your emotions is a great step in moving forward in a healthier way.

Or maybe you are like a friend I have, whose emotions are so big that when he is passionate about something he is talking about, there are usually tears. Or someone whose extreme emotions come out at times, like screaming at your kids for rather small things, because you are stressed or bottle everything else up. Again, working to see your emotional patterns can help.

Q: What do you do when you are stressed and frustrated? Do you keep it in? Talk to someone? Write it down? Do nothing? Blow up? Grab a drink?

Day 78

First Year

Some people aren't good at asking for help because they're so used to being "the helper." Throughout their life they've experienced an unbalanced give and take, so their instinct is usually "I'll figure it out on my own." The self-reliance is all they've ever known.

−Quotes 'nd Notes

This really resonates with me. I'm always quick to say, "It's okay, I'll do it," or "No, I don't need help," when in reality I probably never even took a second to consider whether someone helping me would be beneficial. It can be an automatic response because that is what you have always done. It's hard to change years of the same response in your brain. If this is you, I challenge you to reach out and ask someone for help this week. Yes, it might sound way out of your comfort zone or scary, but it is a good way to exercise your brain.

If you are good with always taking any help, think of someone in your life who might struggle with accepting help. Try to do something for them this week that would help them. And let them know you wanted to do it because you knew they wouldn't ask for help themselves. Maybe this will open them up a bit to accepting help more often or not doing everything themselves.

Q: What can you do this week?

Year +

Expecting things to change without putting in any effort is like waiting for a ship at the airport.

—Bright Vibes

Maybe you have been waiting for things to get better but haven't taken any steps on your own. A lot of people do this with grief. They get wrapped up in everyday lives and don't work on processing their grief—and poof, it's a year or ten years later. I'm guilty of this, but the difference for me is that I started taking steps.

I started writing about what was going on inside. I started going to grief groups and volunteering at kids' grief groups. I went to counseling; I talked to my doctor and was on medication for a bit. I rented books from the library. I started opening up more to my sisters and friends about how I was struggling. The neat thing was, I began to see that I wasn't alone. Others had unprocessed grief years later. It is very common.

Q: What change have you been waiting for? How can you take a small step toward it?

Day 79

First Year

For a seed to achieve its greatest expression, it must come completely undone. The shell cracks, its insides come out and everything changes. To someone who doesn't understand growth, it would look like complete destruction.

—Cynthia Occelli

The way you perceive your current life today may be different from how others would. Some people may feel like the walls are collapsing and their life is completely shattered (which can absolutely be true!). But those outside might see you as the strongest person they know, having seen you vulnerable and surrounded by so much love.

Q: What growth have you seen in your family or in yourself since the death?

Year +

Don't forget to drink water and get some sun. You're basically a houseplant with complicated emotions.

—*Unknown*

Even a year or more later, people can forget to take care of themselves or realize some of their normal self-care might have fallen to the wayside. No joke that today's prompt is about getting outside and drinking water. This could be something you try to do once a day for a week. Drink half your body weight in ounces of water each day, and spend at least ten minutes a day outside. This could even be sitting on your porch or taking your dog for a walk. The movement and getting enough water in your body is a form of self-care.

Q: How many ounces of water do you need to drink today?

I completed my water intake at ____:____ on _____.

Tomorrow I will _____.

Day 80

First Year

You will emerge from this nightmare like the powerful, beautiful, resilient person that you are. It can be hard to remember this when you feel like a shell of the person you once were. But trust me: you are capable of overcoming so much more than you think.

—Elite Daily

What you are going through is not fun. It's probably one of the most challenging things in your life. Take a moment to think about others in your life, or even famous people who have overcome such big challenges, deaths, accidents, and setbacks in their lives. You have the ability to get out of your nightmare and overcome this difficult time. It may not seem like it right now, but you can do it. I believe that *you* can!

At different seasons in my life, I have looked up to different people. After having my daughter, I kept thinking back to someone I knew who didn't have parents after having kids. She went through it and is an amazing person.

Q: Who in your life do you look up to for overcoming some tough obstacles?

Year +

Now, everytime I witness a strong person, I want to know: What darkness did you conquer in your story? Mountains do not rise without earthquakes.

—Katherin MacKenett

The more I meet new people and encounter how strong they are as people, I often wonder what heartache or tough times they've gone through to make them who they are today. Think about the strong people in your life and what they have overcome.

Q: What has gotten in the way of you getting stronger? No faith, fear, confusion, lack of motivation, complacency, victim mentality? Truthfully, what "muscle" do you need to flex to make yourself stronger?

Day 81

First Year

> When thinking about life, remember this: no amount of guilt can change the past, and no amount of anxiety can change the future.
>
> —Unknown

Way easier said than done, right? I carried guilt around for many years after my dad died, for not being home when he died. My mom did the same thing: she had guilt for not being in the room when he actually died because she was on the phone with 911. I always like to share what her counselor told her that she used to share with a lot of people who also struggled with guilt. She said, "Maybe God knew you wouldn't be able to handle it, so he placed you in a different room when it happened!" That made me think! Wow.

Q: What guilty thoughts are you hanging on to? What do you think a best friend, counselor or someone you look up to would say to you? What do you think the person who died would say to you about your guilt?

Year +

> When a flower doesn't bloom, you fix the environment in which it grows, not the flower.
>
> —Alexander Den Heijer

You would add fertilizer or more water to your plant if it was not growing. You wouldn't start taping petals to the stem to make it into a flower, would you? Are you in an environment (physically or mentally) in which you are not allowing yourself to grow? They say the five people you associate with most are the sum of your reality. Do you live with someone who is going through some tough stuff like anxiety or depression? Are you associating with people who only talk about the bad stuff in the world? Or are you hanging out with friends who only consume drugs or alcohol? If you could envision a better environment, what would it look like to you?

Q: If you could envision a better and healthier environment, what would it look like to you?

Day 82

First Year

You can't calm the storm. So stop trying. What you can do is calm yourself. The storm will pass.

—Timber Hawkeye

How does this quote resonate with you? To some it might feel like a struggle to just let things go as is and not control the storm. Some people jump into reading all the books, going full force and finding ways to fix how they are feeling. If that is you, try to take a day to just stop. On purpose don't pick up those books or seek out ways to fix things. Take a day off to see how it feels.

Or are you the opposite where you are just living in the storm and not sure which way to turn? Take some time to scan your current situation from an outside perspective.

Q: What do you need today, to take a break or to take action?

Year +

To the girl who hasn't been herself lately … Your spark will return, and you will shine like you were meant to. It's difficult when you catch yourself not being you. When you feel your whole world falling apart before your eyes.

—Alison, The Minds Journal

Some people say it feels as if they are in a hole trying to climb out, but each day they slip back down, and the hole gets bigger. Other people describe things as looking dull and not very vibrant. Take a moment to think back to when you were happiest as a child. What were you doing—laughing, playing sports, dancing, running around with friends, riding four-wheelers, playing games with family, swimming?

Q: Thinking back to those happy times, how does that make you feel inside? Does something light up thinking about the good clean fun? Now how can you recreate that in your life today? Maybe it's doing one of the things you loved to do as a child and acting goofy, or maybe it's taking time to just take a break, look through old photos, or reminisce about old times with friends and family.

Day 83

First Year

> If your path demands you to walk through Hell, walk as if you own the place.
>
> —Unknown

Some of us are living in what feels like Hell. Your life has been thrown upside down in an instant. It can be your current reality for a while, but just remember, your current situation is not your final destination.

Q: Who can you lean on this week that you haven't reached out to before?

Year +

> You are the artist of your own life, don't hand the paintbrush to anyone else.
>
> —Unknown

If you don't like your current state, change it. Nobody is going to change your life for you, unless something is forced. Your own happiness resides with you. That can be tough to hear if you have been waiting for something or someone to change your happiness. ("I will be happy when …"; "When this happens life will be better …"). Statements like that running through your head indicate that you are the product of not taking action.

Q: What do you want your life to look like? What step can you take this week to make progress in that direction?

Day 84

First Year

Kids are like a mirror, what they see and hear they do. Be a good reflection for them.

−K. Heath

If you have kids around, don't hide your emotions in front of them, because they are going to see you doing that and subconsciously think that is what they need to do too.

If you don't have kids, think of the others around you—spouse, coworkers, friends. How you are reacting to situations can become a learned behavior for others around you.

Q: Are you repeating patterns from how you reacted to things in your childhood or reacting the way your parents would have in your situation?

Year +

Never let the sadness of your past and the fear of your future ruin the happiness of your present.

−Wise Mystic

That is easier said than done, but I do like this quote. I say that because I have dealt with depression and anxiety for a large part of my adult life. Put being a mom on top of that, and I am constantly going between the worlds of past sadness and future worry (about me and my family). Some exercises people do are things like meditation or working out and bringing their bodies to the present moment. There are apps out there that can help with this.

But for some, that seems too woo-woo or foreign. Some exercises you can do and can teach your kids are easy grounding techniques.

- Take a break and count backwards.
- Name five things you can see around you.
- Take a break and take some deep breaths.

Q: What is something you can do long-term to remind yourself to take a moment to be in the present instead of the past or future? (Some examples: wear a worry bracelet, keep a rock in your pocket to remind you each time you put your hand in your pocket, leave a Post-it in your car, and write a message on your mirror.)

Day 85

First Year

Don't get frustrated if it feels like all you're doing is chipping away at something too big for you. That's exactly how masterpieces are eventually made.

—Rigel Dawson

Things can seem overwhelming at times for people going through a new grief journey. Putting one positive foot forward each day can help even if you can't see the big picture. Make sure you carve out some time to mentally list or write out how far you have come.

Q: What have you done since the death that you can say you are proud of?

Year +

Don't compare your Chapter 1 to someone else's Chapter 20.

—Unknown

This is so easy to do; I play this game all the time. I look at where someone is and run all the reasons why I'm not as good through my head. But I don't stop to think that they have had more experience in life or they have had many more years in the field.

The same holds true for grief. I often hear, "So-and-so's husband also died around the same time, and she is doing much better than you." Such a statement takes no account of the reality that a given person's circumstances and coping skills are unique. One who seems far along in the process might have had a lot of family support or different ways to work through the tough times.

Q: Whose Chapter 20 have you been comparing yourself to?

Day 86

First Year

Everything in life starts with your mindset first and your actions second. Your actions follow your thoughts, your beliefs and ideas. To make a shift, to free your energy: start with getting your mind right, and then, take action.

—Unknown

If you took a scan of your mind right now, would you say it's tipping the scale of being more positive or negative? I'm guessing if it is more negative, your current life feels as though it is lacking or things aren't moving forward as you had hoped. Taking action to put your mindset in a healthier place can do wonders to make a shift in your life.

Q: Do you wish a shift would happen in your life?

Year +

Enjoy life now. This is not a rehearsal.

—Unknown

You know this more than most people: life is short. Life is precious, and we are not all guaranteed tomorrow.

Q: If you were told you had two days left to live, what would you do and say to friends and family? If you heard the person closest to you say they had two days left to live, what would you do with them?

Day 87

First Year

The days will always be brighter because he existed. The nights will always be darker because he is gone. And no matter what anybody says about grief, and about time healing all wounds, the truth is, there are certain sorrows that never fade away until the heart stops beating and the last breath is taken.

—Unknown

That is a deep one for sure. It speaks to so many levels of what people go through before, during, and after a death.

Q: If you wrote a book about your experience(s) with the death of loved ones, what would be the biggest theme?

Year +

I wasn't prepared for you to die. People gave me advice for dating and getting married and having babies. But no one prepared me for what it was like to lose the person I loved.

—Learning About Grief

Nobody is ever prepared for death—even if it is a long battle or cancer diagnosis, even if they have gone through a death before. Each experience is unique, and each season in your life is unique.

Q: How would you label the season in your life when your person(s) died? How would you label the season in your life today?

Day 88

First Year

At the start of each day, there is a moment that I realize that there is a part of me missing. Sometimes it's manageable and sometimes it's not. I've been asked many times to describe what it is that I feel and it's like never being able to find home again. Yet I yearn just to be home one more time. This is grief and loss.

__Unknown

This is super powerful to me. In a way it is spot-on metaphorically and actually. After my mom died, we had to sell my parents' house, and it was super tough. I never had that feeling of home again.

Q: What is a way you would describe grief and loss?

Year +

Speak their name. Someone I love has gone away. And life is not the same. The greatest gift that you can give is just to speak their name. I need to hear the stories and the tales of days gone past. I need for you to understand these memories must last. We cannot make more memories. Since they're no longer here. So when you speak of them to me it's music to my ear.

–Out of the Ashes

I love, love, love hearing stories from people (some I know and some I don't) about my parents. It is almost as if their spirit comes alive for a moment. At first this might still hurt, with sadness and an ache at hearing such stories, but as time goes on, you will find comfort in hearing their name, seeing their photos, and hearing stories. Remember, others are out there just waiting for you to tell a story about a loved one who has died.

Q: Can you reach out to someone this week to share a story or fun memory?

Day 90

First Year

> You won't ever be your old self again … You are growing into a new self. A new self that is born out of that grief.
>
> —Ashley Davis Bush

It might be hard to admit, but you won't ever be the same as before. The way you perceive this can mean a lot. Some people are bitter about it and can't move past it. This is where they get stuck in their grief journey. For some it lasts months or even years.

Others just don't want to be a new person, because that means moving on without the person who died—and that is a tough reality to live in. (Not to mention the sadness.)

Sometimes people move into this new self and don't even realize it. All of a sudden you blink, and you are not the same person you were "before."

Q: How would you explain to someone else today what you have grown into … or hope to grow into?

Year +

> I don't care who is doing better than me. I am doing better than I was last year. It's me vs me.
>
> —Jess

This can be easy for some and hard for others. For me it is tough. I always compare unintentionally. If I remind myself to look at where I was a year ago or a few years ago, then I actually realize how far I have come.

Q: Are you better off in certain areas in your life than last year? Are you struggling in certain areas compared to last year? (The goal is to be honest with yourself on this.)

Monthly Exercises

This section is intended to educate you on topics surrounding grief and to help you work through some common topics. The goal is to expand the way you look at things. Again, my hope for you is to be completely honest when working through the exercises.

January
Where is your loved one?

This is a great question to ask yourself as time goes on. I don't mean where are they buried or where is the urn. I'm talking about something different. When you think about the person who died, take some time, and think about what you see. Read each question; then close your eyes.

1. Where are they? (location) _____
   _____
   _____

2. What are they doing? (action) _____
   _____
   _____

3. What are they wearing? (appearance) _____
   _____
   _____

How you answer these questions can say a lot about you.

For the first question: If they are at the scene of an accident or some place that has caused you trauma, you most likely are stuck and need to seek help processing your trauma. If they are sitting on the couch in your childhood home, you could be fixating on the past and miss them in the present. If you see them doing something with you in the future, you could be at a good point in your life where you see them walking alongside you in your journey on this earth. Take some time to think about where you are seeing your loved one. There might be something there that could help you.

For the second question: Take some time to reflect on this one as well. Is it tipped more toward something positive or negative? Do they look happy, angry, sad, confused, suffering, content, joyful? This could reveal how you feel about their death or show some red flags as to where you are stuck. Set a timer for five minutes to sit with this one, think through it, and write it out. Talk to someone you trust to get their input. The goal is to be truthful as to what you learn.

For the third question: Appearance can also be clues into your hurting or healing. Were you seeing bold colors, or was everything pretty drab? That could be a clue into your mood when you think of the person who died. Was your person dressed in nice clothes, wearing regular everyday clothes, or dirty and not looking so good? This could be another indication of your current mood or feelings toward your person. Again, take some time to think through what you are seeing and what it could unveil.

This exercise is great to do when you are feeling lost or after more time has passed. The more you work on your healing, the more you might surprise yourself on where your person is when you think of them.

February
Struggling

We choose to heal and we choose to move forward by being brave and vulnerable enough to heal.

−Desmond Tutu

This is a topic that is near and dear to my heart. The main reason is because it is raw and real, and not many people actually talk about it. Yet most people around you are struggling with something in their lives. It is an isolating feeling when you feel alone in your struggles.

By struggling, I mean a variety of ways: with mental health, depression, and anxiety; or with grief and struggling with how to handle your feelings or help others with theirs; the feeling of loneliness; physical, sexual, or verbal abuse; or struggling with a divorce (either your parents' or your own), or even struggling financially; struggles internally with a spouse who doesn't communicate; struggling to conceive, or even struggling because everyone around you is married and you are not.

Almost everyone you interact with in your day is probably struggling with something, but we don't openly talk about it for many reasons.

Some facts:

- "42 million adults in the United States live with an anxiety disorder" (Nami).
- "Each year, about 2.5 million people die nationwide. Every death leaves behind an average of 4 or 5 grieving survivors" (GB Health Watch).
- "There is 1 divorce approximately every 36 seconds. That's nearly 2,400 divorces per day, 16,800 divorces per week and 876,000 divorces a year. The divorce rate for a first marriage is around 41%" (Hampton Roads Legal).
- "The average American household has $16K in credit card debt" (Our Debt Free Family).
- "More than 60% of lonely people are married. When married couples no longer share their deepest feelings, thoughts, and experiences with one another it can leave them feeling disconnected and alone" (*Psychology Today*).

Reading those statistics really goes to show that most adults are walking around struggling in some shape or way. If they are struggling and not dealing with it in a healthy way, their kids (or others in their life) may mimic how they deal with life's struggles. It is a trickling effect.

One thing I know is you can't make people seek help. A person will look for healing or help when they want to. Healing and help can come from something as simple as setting different boundaries and limits. Instead of working until you are exhausted, maybe you schedule some time with your family. Instead of not communicating with your spouse, maybe write them an email.

There are many things you can do. Another idea is to validate your feelings. You may want to join an online group or forum. Most are anonymous, and you can let all your worries out and connect with others. Or join an in-person group about what you are struggling with. Talk to your doctor if it is mental health–related, or schedule a counseling appointment. (As I said, nobody can nudge you to do these things).

Remember that what you allow yourself is what kids (or others in your life) might allow too. Do you want your kids to pick up the same pattern of stuffing feelings down or learn how not to communicate? Do you want them to pick up on patterns of depression and think that is the way every parent lives?

The purpose of this section is to let you know you are not alone. Others are out there struggling too. You can choose to stay where you are. You can choose to connect with others who are struggling. You can choose to let it out in healthy ways. Or you can choose to cope in unhealthy ways. Either way, nobody else can make that decision; it is yours.

Try to respond to the statements below *truthfully*:

1.	As of today I think I have done a good job at working through my grief.	Yes	No
2.	I feel like I have someone to talk to about my struggles right now.	Yes	No
3.	Lately, I reach out or cope in healthy ways when I'm struggling.	Yes	No
4.	I have a good pattern of expressing my feelings in a healthy way.	Yes	No
5.	I practice healthy coping skills.	Yes	No
6.	I can't remember the last time I cried.	Yes	No
7.	I am usually stressed about something.	Yes	No
8.	I'd rather keep everything to myself instead of bothering others.	Yes	No
9.	I feel shame or guilt around my struggles.	Yes	No
10.	Someone has suggested that I seek help for my struggles.	Yes	No

11. Currently I am struggling with:

_____

_____

_____

_____

_____

Reflection:

If you answered mostly Yes in 1 through 5, you are on a great path.

If you answered mostly Yes in 6 through 10, you might want to take a step in connecting with others (doctor, counselor, professionals, chaplain, support groups), or try some healthy coping skills.

Action item: Truthfully, how do you feel about where you are right now with your struggles? What action do you know you *should* take, but haven't taken that step yet?

An action plan: Be bold and take that step. Or dip your toe in the water and talk to someone about what you are struggling with. Or you could also think about *why* you haven't taken a step yet. What is holding you back?

March
Trauma

An estimated 90 percent of adults in the United States have experienced a traumatic event at least once in their lives.

—Psychology Today

Don't skip over this topic, even if you think you haven't experienced trauma. It is meant to educate you on what trauma really is, what it looks like, and the effects of it in our bodies and on those around us. We are going deep today with this topic because it is not a topic openly discussed in our culture.

Most people think of trauma as some big horrific tragedy like a kidnapping, murder, accident, or paralysis, but it can be far broader than that.

Definition of trauma: An intense event that causes harm to your physical or emotional well-being (kidsmentalhealthinfo.com).

> It's important to note that it isn't necessarily the specific nature of the death that makes it traumatic, rather how the event is interpreted and experienced by the individual. One cannot underestimate the impact of personal factors like emotional regulation, cognitive responses, secondary stressors, coping style, prior history of trauma, and access to support and resources in determining how a person responds to an event.

—What's Your Grief

Even the death of a loved one can be a traumatic event, and most people do not realize it.

Three kinds of trauma:

1. Acute (one event in time)
2. Chronic (repeated and/or prolonged)
3. Complex (multiple events)

Effects of trauma in our bodies:

- Startle easily
- Difficulty concentrating
- Edginess
- Muscle stiffness
- Insomnia

Our responses to trauma:

- Shock
- Denial
- Anger
- Disbelief
- Anxiety

A lot of people refuse to identify and even deal with trauma because they don't know it actually exists. Being educated about trauma can help you or even your child or loved one. Pushing it away or not dealing with it doesn't change the fact that it happened and you went through a traumatic event. If you decide to acknowledge it and process the emotions, healing can happen. It is possible.

Trauma can do a number on our bodies, as you can see from the list above. When you hold on to that much of an emotional burden, it can come out in other ways, such as anger, lashing out at people you love, or even blocking love or refusing to receive.

Learning to process your emotions and work through the past can benefit you as well as your family.

Disclaimer: this is not meant to treat or diagnose anyone. Please consult your healthcare professional with questions or concerns.

April
Regrowth

Don't Irythe concept of change scares you, as much as the concept of staying unhappy.

—Timber Hawkeye

We go through a lot of different seasons in our life. The same is true with a grief journey. Sometimes it is necessary to let go of things that may be holding us back to move forward into a new season. This is mimicked in the seasons in our climate. In order for a flower to bloom, it starts as a seed; then it breaks through the ground, and finally it blossoms. These flowers can't live through a harsh winter, so they must go back into the earth and grow again. A change takes place for regrowth to happen.

The season of regrowth in spring is a beautiful time. Grass becomes green again, flowers bloom, birds migrate back, trees bud flowers, baby animals are born. Seemingly infinite change and regrowth happens. Imagine if our world around us stayed cooler, muddy, with brown or yellow grass, no birds chirping, bare trees, gloomy skies, and no new animals. It's a pretty dark, sad, and low feeling, isn't it? That is how a lot of people feel after a death. Some people stay in this state of mind and emotional and physical feeling for a long time.

It isn't until a person makes a decision to move past the grayness that any change and regrowth can happen. For some people, it is just a natural progression that happens, and they may start to heal faster and move through their grief right away. Others can be in this state for months and even years without realizing it. Many people don't change because they are uncomfortable or uneasy and are scared to be vulnerable and actually show emotions. But growth can be beautiful, like the renewal of spring.

Nobody can make you grow or change. It is something that is a choice that only you can make when you are ready, or when your current state is not acceptable to you anymore. Then wonderful things can happen. "Be like a flower, survive the rain but use it to grow" (Unknown).

You can move forward after a tough death! It is possible. I have seen it happen for hundreds of people in really hard circumstances and tragic losses. The main reason why they decided to take a step in their healing journey was either that they wanted to feel better than their current state or that they wanted to use their tough loss to help others. In both situations, people made a choice to grow into a new season of their life—a happier one and a more meaningful one.

This might sound wonderful and like shiny roses, but how do you do this, or where do you turn? I recently heard someone say, "We grieve like we live our lives. If you don't know what to do in situations, you do what you know." I love this because it is true! Nobody is taught how to grieve or how to go through a death. So by default we as humans do what we know. For a lot of people, that is to suppress feelings and bottle them up.

Depending on what you like there are many resources available out there or even things you can do on your own.

If you like to keep to yourself, you might look for grief or personal development books if you like to read, or podcasts and videos if you like to listen. Try just writing or typing what is going on in your life on a piece of paper or device. You could try looking on YouTube for a video or meditation specific to grief as well. The cool thing is that if you are apprehensive about taking a step into something new, you can try these things without anyone knowing.

If you like to connect with other people, you might want to reach out to someone you know who has gone through a similar death. Or look for a grief group in your area or online. Circles is a great app that connects people with others who have gone through similar loss.

If you are more closed off to talking to a group, but would try something one-on-one, reach out to a counselor or a local funeral home; connect with a grief group that might have individual connections or with your local church.

If you are looking for a baby step into growing in your grief journey, try something like looking at pictures of your loved one. Or you could play their favorite song and jot down some notes about what was going on inside you while you listened to it. If you have been avoiding crying, watch a movie that you know will make you emotional. If you want to work out some anger, try something physical like kickboxing, axe throwing, finding a smash room, or punching a pillow.

Some of these (or all) might sound uncomfortable or out of your comfort zone. That is probably the reason why you haven't taken a step to move forward, because it doesn't feel comfortable or easy. *Change takes a bit of courage and work. But just like the spring, wonderful things can come from it.* Be that flower that fights to get through the earth, because no matter what, you will grow from it. Even if you try something and realize it is not for you, you took a step and learned what won't work for you right now. Maybe it is something that will help you later in life, but right now it is not your cup of tea.

I've read lots of books, listened to many podcasts, and tried journaling—almost to the point of forcing myself because everyone says journaling works wonders. I've looked into mindfulness, writing, and meditation. I've learned what really makes me think and process my emotions *right now* in my life and what doesn't do much for me.

Once you learn what is helping you grow, *do more of that when it feels right.* For me, I'll take a meditation and journaling or yoga and journaling class (virtual or in person) a few times a year. I get *a lot* out of those! I tried doing meditation and yoga on my own at home with an app, and I couldn't get in the right headspace for it. Maybe someday it will be what I need in my life, but it doesn't seem to help me right now. I used to love kickboxing in the morning and would see a counselor a few times a month, but both are not something I feel I need in my life right now. So right now for me (in this season of my life), I'll stick with doing some journaling classes, retreats, writing, going to an adult grief group, and reading books for my personal development and healing journey.

Try something, and do what works for you. Don't force what other people tell you will help.

Action: Think about how you like to spend your time. Is it alone? With a few people? With groups of people? Use that information to reflect on and try something new in association with how you like to spend your time.

May
Bleeding Heart

I've lived through this a few times in my life now. I've seen friends and family members do so as well. My guess is you are like me, and you too have lived through one of the worst days of your life, the day they died. For me, my world stopped, but everyone else's world did not.

My heart has been bleeding for the past twelve years, but it has been slowly repairing the more I've done the work. By doing the work, I mean working through my grief. I'm a thinker; I like to process things by connecting the dots, getting answers, and understanding how things work. Not everyone is like me, and that's why there are so many different programs out there. After my dad died when I was in college, I pushed my emotions to the side. I ignored my sadness, loneliness, depression, anxiety—and grief. It wasn't until five years later, when my mom unexpectedly died, that I realized I had never dealt with my grief.

I grew up pushing my feelings down and not processing them. So that is what I did with grief. How was I supposed to know that would come back to snowball my grief? It was after my mom died that I decided to go to an in-person grief group. I told my story to complete strangers, and I cried! It had been years and years since I cried over the death of my dad. I thought about him every day and still do, but I kept my emotions at bay. Who wants to cry? Little did I know my heart was bleeding all those years, and I didn't acknowledge it.

I started reading books about grief. I started looking up grief groups on Facebook and connecting with friends who had also lost a parent. Then I reached out to a counselor because I realized how crappy I really was feeling all those years. I also started writing about my grief. We all process emotions and grief differently. We are all unique, just like our grief. Our hearts bleed at different paces and different amounts.

My hope for you is that you'll take some time to analyze whether you are ignoring your bleeding heart. Some people jump right into processing their grief; others are in a numb phase, and it takes a while to get out of the fog. Whenever that time comes when you are ready to try something new to work through your grief, just remember to be proud of yourself.

Action item: Here is an exercise to take a baby step into something new:

Do one thing different each day for five days.

Take a new route to work. Listen to a different genre of music in your car. Turn the TV off this evening for one hour. Go take a walk outside. Make an appointment with a counselor. Take a shower in the morning instead of at night. Use a different shampoo. Write someone a letter. Do a five-minute yoga video. Strike up a conversation with someone in the grocery store. Try kickboxing. Get a massage. Call a friend you haven't talked to in a while (call, not text). Try a new recipe. Check out something at the library. Donate to a charity. Try journaling. Watch the movie you have been avoiding. Look up grief resources in your area. Send someone flowers. Eat with your nondominant hand. Go to a shooting range or ax-throwing place.

The point behind this exercise is to get you out of your routine (and possibly your comfort zone). When you do this, your brain experiences new things and breaks your patterns and habits for a short time. You might learn something about yourself or even try something that might help you.

You can't change your current reality if you don't try.

Today I will:

_____

Tomorrow I will:

_____

The third day I will:

_____

The next day I will:

_____

The day after that I will:

_____

Things I learned or got out of this experience:

_____

June
Guilt and Forgiveness

It is important to point out the difference between guilt and forgiveness.

"Guilt is the *feeling* of being responsible or regretful for a perceived offense, real or imaginary" (Mayo Clinic).

"Forgiveness is the *release* of resentment or anger. Forgiveness doesn't necessarily mean reconciliation" (psychologytoday.com).

There may be things, ideas, expectations or hope you are holding on to that you cannot let go or forgive. This section will walk you through an exercise designed to help you work through the topic of forgiveness. Feel free to think through this section, or type, write, or draw out your answers. The goal is to be honest about it and not dull down your feelings.

1. Make a list of all the things you wish you could forgive yourself for. Look at all areas of your life:
   a. Work/school
   b. Home life
   c. Relationships
   d. Money
   e. Your health
   f. Grief/death
   g. Your emotions
2. Circle one that you want to focus on.
3. Take time to think about all the reasons why you think this is true. Where did this feeling stem from? When did you first start feeling this root emotion?
4. Did this serve a purpose at one point in your life?
5. Is there a new story you can tell yourself?

Looking at forgiveness as something you would like to get over can be limiting. If you look at it from a place that it served you at one point in your life, it can help some people move on from it.

Action item: Spend some time with this topic by writing yourself a letter apologizing for letting it hurt you, but talk about how you will work on this going forward. Finish the letter by saying you forgive yourself, and be thankful for serving its purpose in your life at one point. The next few pages have worksheets to help you work through these items.

July
Compounding Grief + Timeline

Maybe this sounds like you, or you may know someone who has experienced a story like this:

At the end of 2008 my grandma died right before Christmas. It was the first big family funeral that hit me hard. A few months later my dad died, and that hit me like a ton of bricks. I didn't do well with the death and pushed my emotions aside to "get through" life and "move on." A little while later I had a friend die, and then a few years later my mom died. I write this not to talk about tally marks of death to explain compound grief, but to explain that death over a lifetime can create a snowball effect.

The phrase *compound grief* really is a way to explain tangled grief accumulated over a lifetime. I didn't deal with the emotions and the loss of my grandma; then my dad died right afterward, and I avoided everything that reminded me of him. Even not reacting to a death is a choice. I was unintentionally choosing not to deal with the pain I was feeling. Who really wants to feel horrible and sad?

I wanted to talk about this topic not to give you a textbook term for maybe something you are going through, but to open your eyes to the thought of it being something others are doing as well. To talk about this term is not to shame anyone for acting this way; however, a lot of people's first instinct is to try not to feel deep sadness and move on with life. Being aware of what you might unintentionally be doing by not leaning into your grief is the first step.

The term *cumulative loss* is pretty similar. It means many losses over time. Some examples may be:

- Multiple deaths over time
- Multiple pet deaths
- Death and other losses over time (loss of job, loss of income, loss of home, etc.)
- Multiple losses over time

After my mom died, we had to sell my childhood home. This was so stinking tough, it was like grieving the loss of a person. The emotions hit me pretty hard. What I didn't realize was that I *was* actually grieving the loss of that house. It was another added loss to my life. So my hope for you is that this opens your eyes a bit to help realize your grief is complicated, but working on it in pieces can help you in your healing journey.

Try not to think of yourself as having gone through a number of deaths or losses and feeling like a victim. Instead, realize that each one has made you who you are today and can help you grow into a stronger person. Each loss can be worked on as an individual loss and not an overall grief.

Timeline Exercise

You are about to work through a powerful exercise that may seem like it would be meant for younger kids, but anyone can work through this at any age. We are going to map out your life. This is a way to make your past into a visual so you may see in front of you all the different changes you have gone through, throughout your life.

1. Take out a piece of blank paper and draw a horizontal line.
2. On the far left side, put your birth date.
3. On the far right, write "today" and the date, then continue the line farther to the right or below your line.
4. As you move to the right, make a mark with any big events in your life. Some ideas are listed below.
5. Then where you have gone through a death, on your timeline make a bar straight up for each death. The taller the bar, the more intense the loss was.
6. For each item on your timeline put a + where it was a positive event, and - where it was a negative event.
7. Get out a bright color and review your timeline. Think about which one or ones still seem unresolved or unfinished to you. Highlight those on your timeline.
8. Make notes if you can identify any stages or turning points in your life.
9. Lastly, write out what each event taught you.
10. Keep this somewhere safe, and revisit it when new events in your life occur to continue your timeline and learnings in your life.

Born   Today

(DATE)_____|__|_____|_____|_____|____|__|__|__|__ (DATE)

Ideas:

Getting a new pet

Big birthday you remember

Starting a new school

Moving house

Birth of sibling, kids, grandkids

New friends

Death of pet, friend, family member

Car accidents

Accidents

Big life events

Joining groups

Volunteer work

Relationships

Armed forces

Diagnosis in the family

Marriage, Divorce

Trips/Vacations

Awards

Graduation from schools

Degrees, certificates, achievements

Got driver's license or lost license

Tickets or jail (you or family members)

New cars

Celebrations

Jobs - starting, stopping

Attending something new

Change in family structure

Attack/Trauma/Abuse

Mental health issues

Notes:

_____

August
Finding Meaning

Most people do not realize the largeness of grief until they go through a death. So many different emotions can come into play that you may not expect. Some people wonder, *Why did this happen?* or *What am I supposed to learn from this death?* or *Is there something I can do now because of this death to help others?*—all for the sole purpose of finding meaning out of death.

There is a TEDx talk by Justin Yopp called "More Than Grief." It talks about how seven fathers joined a grief support group and their journey through it. To me it is very interesting to hear how they were able to lean on each other and grow through their grief together. Justin talks about three things they learned from going to the group:

1. They learned to reimagine a new life without the person who died.
2. They searched to find meaning out of the death.
3. They needed to connect to others who went through a similar loss.

Book recommendations:

Finding Meaning: The Sixth Stage of Grief by David Kessler, a longtime grief specialist. The book is great if you are looking to dive deep into understanding how people process emotions and grief, and why finding meaning from death is important. There is also a podcast called On Grief & Finding Meaning that is great to listen to in your car or at home or if you put some headphones on while you take a walk or workout. Brené Brown is a great author and speaker. She teamed up with David Kessler to produce this podcast on the same topic as his book. It's pretty neat in my opinion.

Option B by Sheryl Sandberg. This book is about a wife whose husband died, and they navigate through life with the mentality of Option B. Option A would be that dad is here, but Option B is what we have to look at. It is a great book, and it talks through the meaning of their new roles as a family and what life is like after a major loss.

One widow used the analogy of her life as a puzzle. Before the accident, she was married and had two small children. She knew where she was going; the puzzle of her life was almost complete. Then when the mine exploded and she lost her husband, she said it was as if somebody had picked up her puzzle and thrown it on the floor. From that point on, her life was about putting it back together, but she only had half the pieces. She was adamant that she was going to reassemble her puzzle.

The pieces she had left made a different picture. The life she had before was no longer possible. But she was motivated to pick up the pieces to make something new. It took time. It involved small steps. But she believed it was possible for her to live a full life again.

Action item: Take some time to think about the questions below. If you have kids or close family members who share a death with you, think about opening up and asking them one or two of the questions below. Writing down your answers can be helpful, because what you answer today might look different a year or ten years from now.

Questions:

Have you thought about why this event happened in your life?

What do you think going through a death in your life has shown you or made you realize?

Do you see your life as more precious or fragile than before death?

Have you seen a friend or family member struggle with the loss of the person who died?

If so, how has their life changed since the death?

Is there a place for you to be of support to that friend or family member?

Do you think there is a reason you were there for the last moments of life (or you were not there)?

What have you learned through the pain, hurt, or anger of the death?

How are you a better person because of the loss?

September
Gratitude

Gratitude helps people feel more positive emotions, relish good experiences, improve their health, deal with adversity, and build strong relationships. People feel and express gratitude in multiple ways.

—Harvard Health

This is one of my favorite topics, mainly because I have seen the magic behind it. You might be wondering why an adult grief booklet would be talking about being grateful when my favorite person just died or when I'm still hurting so much over the loss. This section is meant for you to take a step back from focusing on death and to dig deep to find gratitude in your life. You might have to dig, and that is okay. There are books out there that can help you walk through a practice.

I read a book and went through the exercises twice; it really helped me realize how much in my life I should be grateful for. The book is called *The Magic* by Rhonda Byrne. It is a twenty-eight-day journey of journaling and activities centered around gratitude.

I notice in my life that when I focus on gratitude, things shift for me mentally in a good way. There are guided gratitude journals out there as well that can help you through thinking about gratitude prompts. Most are designed for about five minutes a day to help you keep up the habit of writing. Or some people just grab their computer or a notebook and write out five things a day they are grateful for. After about day 3 you might start really reaching and searching deep for things to be grateful for. It is a pretty neat practice because when was the last time you felt truly grateful for your legs? But if later today you were in a cast up to your hip because you broke your leg, you would be so stinking grateful the day you get that cast off and can walk again and shower by yourself again.

The benefits of practicing gratitude are nearly endless. People who regularly practice gratitude by taking time to notice and reflect upon the things they're thankful for experience more positive emotions, feel more alive, sleep better, express more compassion and kindness, and even have stronger immune systems.

Here are a few more ideas on how to practice gratitude daily:

- Gratitude journaling
- Gratitude board (visual pictures of what you are grateful for)
- Gratitude jar (write on a piece of paper what you are grateful for)
- Gratitude meditation (apps out there or YouTube videos)

A good structure for writing out gratitude is to say what you are grateful for. Think about what it would feel like not to have that in your life. Write down why you are grateful for that "thing," and really think about it; then say thank you with lots of appreciation. Doing this small exercise causes you to think about the why and really show appreciation to the thing you are grateful for. It might look something like this:

I am grateful for _____ because _____. Thank you, thank you, thank you!

I am so extremely grateful for _____ because _____. Thank you, thank you, thank you!

I am truly blessed to have _____ in my life, because _____ . Thank you, thank you, thank you!

I hold gratitude for _____ because _____. Thank you, thank you, thank you!

I appreciate _____ in my life, because _____. If it was not in my life, my life would be different in the following ways: _____

Thank you, thank you, thank you!

Action item: Commit to five days of something around gratitude. This could be anything listed above or an idea you have. Reflect back on if your mood or anything is different after these few days.

October
Unprocessed Grief

It only takes one person to make you happy and change your life: *you.*

—iliketoquote.com

This can happen to many people and they don't even know it. It might seem like you are doing just fine because you don't cry or get bothered by things, but do any of the items below ring true to you?

- You don't want to talk about the death.
- You push memories or their things out of sight because it is painful.
- You avoid any groups, counseling, or education on grief because it would be painful.
- You avoid places that remind you of that person.
- You only fixate on their positives, avoiding their negatives, or vice versa.
- You put up a wall for others and shut down when topics about death come up.
- You obsess over the person who died, which consumes your mind.
- You consume drugs or alcohol to unwind or avoid feelings.
- You constantly need to be busy—when downtime causes anxiety.
- You have a running list of things you want to buy, and shop online or in a store most days.
- You avoid movies that you think will make you cry.

People who have gone through a tough death three months ago can have unprocessed grief. The same is true with someone who lost a loved one twenty or more years ago. There is no shame in this. Many of us grew up sweeping feelings under the rug, because that is what our parents taught us to do.

If you have unprocessed grief, there are a number of steps you could take to dig into the loss.

Ways you can take a step in processing your grief:

Seek out a grief counselor

Join a grief group

Start a journal and write or draw out what is going on

Do something in memory of your loved one

Rent a grief book, listen to a grief podcast, or do grief meditation

Connect with others who have gone through a similar loss. (Look up Circles in your app store)

Talk to your doctor/counselor/physician about suggestions and resources if you are feeling depressed, have anxiety, or suffer from past trauma.

Action item: One thing I realized (or am going to do) is _____

November
Grief during the Holidays

The reality is there will always be a "holiday." This topic comes up more toward the end of the year, though, with Thanksgiving and Christmas being large friends-and-family-oriented holidays. Some tips that "What's Your Grief" wrote about last year are still my favorite go-to helpful guidelines for holidays.

Practical Plan for Holidays

1. *Anticipate what the day(s) will look like.* Sometimes the anxiety leading up to the holiday is far worse than the actual day. Think through who you would like to spend the day with.

2. *Decide what "tradition" means.* Think through how this year is going to look different. If you are going to be skipping a house visit or an event that you typically do, think through whether you want to do a modified tradition or—if it's too painful this year—how you feel about skipping the "tradition" this year.

3. *Did any roles change?* Is one person taking on the missing role this holiday, or hosting the holiday/meal? It might be a great way to "busy" yourself, but be conscious of that new weight on their shoulders, and maybe offer to help. A good way to approach this could be to tell them you were thinking about bringing XYZ, and ask if that is okay. If you ask what they want help with, the short answer might be that they have it covered.

4. *Talk to kids about the holiday.* Make sure they are in the loop of how the holiday might be different this year. At any age, from two to fifty-two, it can be a mixture of feelings, and some kids might be feeling guilty about being excited or happy about events coming up but still sad or lonely at the same time. If you keep them in the loop about this year's "holiday plan," it opens things up for discussion, or at the very least they will feel included.

5. *Plan for breakdowns.* That Johnny Cash song or Christmas carol might come on the radio when you are in the middle of shopping for a present and could trigger a breakdown. Plan ahead: put tissues in your purse, keep some Tic Tac in your car, carry a second set of makeup.

6. *Incorporate the person who died into your holiday.* This could be done in a number of ways. Buy them a present and donate it to a shelter or Toys for Tots. Or write them a letter during the holiday. See below for some more ideas.

Meal Holiday Ideas

1. *Create a special tablecloth:* This is a neat idea to use every year. Find a durable tablecloth that you can write on. Every meal that this tablecloth is used for, each person gets to sign and date their name. It's neat to look back every year at who was there, who is missing, but know that they are still with you at the table.

2. *Have a favorite meal:* This can be done before or after the actual holiday. Turn it into a theme night. For instance, if the departed person liked German food, go to a German restaurant or make a German food night. Another idea is that everyone makes something that they remember the loved one liking. A therapist suggested this to a family once, and the fun part was the meal was so random it created a lot of joy for the families. They had tacos, bowls of candy, hot sticks, punch, sweet and sour soup, caramel apples, popcorn, and fudge. This could be such a fun idea.

Gift Giving Holiday Idea

1. *Thankful present:* Invite family and friends to take part in this idea. Think about the most meaningful or important thing you received from the person who died. This could be something intangible (love, hope, forgiveness, kindness) or a special present. On a piece of paper, write this or a symbol that represents this gift. Wrap your "present." This is the first gift everyone opens. It is a reminder that the person left a legacy; they are still giving gifts even if they are not physically there with you.

2. *Buy them a gift:* You could still buy that person a gift and hold on to it. Or buy one and donate it to a homeless shelter, community center, or Toys for Tots program. Another idea would be to pick a specific charity to donate to in their memory.

December
Grief Myths and Facts

You might have believed some of these myths before you went through a tough death. They are myths that a lot of people feel to be true about death or the grieving process. My goal with this section is that you come to understand that you are not alone; *everything you are feeling and experiencing is okay.* There is no correct way to grieve; everyone's journey is different—just like the relationship you had with your loved one was different from everyone else's relationship with them.

If you keep hearing that record of "What's wrong with me?" or "Why am I not …?" you may not come to a place where you can start healing. The more you are able to see that what you are going through *is* normal, the more you can heal and help others heal.

Myth: Grief is the same thing as sadness.
Truth: Grief is not just *one* emotion or feeling; it is complex and can come in many forms.

> Besides experiencing a mix of feelings like sadness, anger, regret, longing, guilt, and loneliness, we may also experience mood swings. All of that intensity can feel unrelenting and frightening. We may even secretly wonder if we are going crazy. Grief at its most intense can feel that way, as we are thrown off balance by trying to manage so many emotions all at once.
>
> —TAPS Organization

Myth: Everyone follows a similar grief path and timeline.
Truth: Every person's grief path is different. Even if you have lost the same person in your life as others, your path will be different from all others.

> Never have I ever heard a bereaved person exclaim, "Grief is just as expected it to be!"
>
> —What's Your Grief

Myth: Grief will not change your relationships.
Truth: Grief can change the dynamic of a relationship with friends, family, and even a spouse.

> People who grieve can start to feel alone in what they are going through, even if they are married. Being open with people about how you are doing can keep the lines of communication open.

—Grief In Common

Myth: You will or should grieve less when you have warning someone is going to die.
Truth: A loss is a loss.

> Knowing that a person is sick or a lengthy battle with cancer does not mean that the loss of a person will be easy. Grief is hard, grief is tough and a loss is a loss.

—Health at Harvard

Myth: If you haven't gotten rid of your loved one's belongings after X number of years, it means you are not healing.
Truth: People's belongings can bring comfort and healing to some. On the other hand, some people decide to get rid of their belongings, and that brings them comfort and healing.

> There is no right or wrong way to deal with grief.
> Every person is different.
> Every situation is different.
> Every relationship is different.
> Every grief journey is different.
> And that is ok!

—*Psychology Today*

Myth: Grief has an end point
Truth: Your grief journey will last a lifetime. But it can get easier as time passes and as you work through your feelings.

Some people choose to:

- Talk to a counselor
- Join a grief group
- Talk to friends/family
- Journal/write
- Work out/run
- Read self development/grief books
- Listen to music or podcasts
- Look at old pictures
- Tell stories about the person who died

What has helped you in your grief journey?

–Mindfulness and Grief

Myth: The pain after the death of a loved one will go away faster if you just ignore it.
Truth: Trying to ignore the sadness and pain or keeping it unexpressed can make it worse down the road. For real healing, you will need to come face to face with your grief and actively deal with it.

People face their grief head-on in a number of ways. If you are looking to speak to a person, you can work with a counseling program or therapist's office, join grief support groups, confide in your church, and reach out to others who have a background in grief support. Others turn inward and work through their emotions through art, journaling, reading ….

There is no right or wrong way. The only way to not move forward is to shove it all down and not deal with it.

–Huff Post

Myth: If you do not cry, it usually means you are not sorry about the death of a loved one.
Truth: Crying is a normal human response to sadness. People who do not cry may feel the sadness as deeply as others, but internalize or show it in other ways. Everyone's reactions and responses to a situation are going to be different. If someone is not crying (or if you are not crying), it is not wrong. It may be shock, delayed emotions, numbness, or many other reasons.

–It's Ok Not to Cry

Myth: Grieving should last about a year.

Truth: There is no specific time frame for grief. The grief journey will differ for each person. Some people do a lot of processing the first year, but others are numb to reality or shove all the feelings down. It is completely different for each person and each situation.

After my dad died, I didn't really process anything until about five years later, when my mom died. Then it really hit me, and I realized I was avoiding feelings, conversations, and *all* the emotions. I was always a be-"tough"-and-don't-cry type of person.

Action item: Share something you learned about grief with someone else this week. Maybe it is a myth that you thought to be true, or you could tell another person about this booklet, or even something you have learned about yourself and your grief journey since the death.

About the Author

Gina graduated from Seymour, Wisconsin, High School in 2003. She then went on to complete her bachelor's degree and master's degree from. She also holds her Grief Support Specialist Certification from UW-Madison.

Gina, along with some of her peers, started a nonprofit in 2018 called Hope's House in the greater Green Bay area that focuses on free grief support for kids ages 4–18 and their families. Hope's House also provides schools with training to implement a grief support group in their districts. She is currently the executive director.

Gina has written and published a grief book called *It's Ok Not to Cry* based on her own life story and the story of others who have gone through a tough death. After going through the death of her parents when she was in her twenties and numerous other deaths among friends and family members, she started on a path to helping others find hope in dark times. Gina is also the grief support specialist at a funeral home.

Gina loves helping others any way she can. She was awarded the WPS Volunteer of the Year Award in Leadership in 2020 for her work with Hope's House. She also is a volunteer at Camp HOPE, a camp for grieving children in the Stevens Point area. Gina volunteered at the Boys and Girls Club-Fox Valley Center for Grieving Children for a number of years and was a hospice volunteer through Aurora at Home Hospice.

In 2021 she developed an online program for those wanting to seek healing for grief on their own time. Grief Your Way is a tailored grief program based on an assessment that covers relationship to the deceased, behavior, and some psychology (www.griefyourway.com). Each person gets their own grief plan to work through at their own pace. You are also able to connect one-on-one online with an expert in any field you choose: anxiety, depression, aromatherapy, etc.

When Gina is not working she enjoys reading and spending time up at her cabin with her family and friends.

> The greatest good is what we do for one another.
>
> —Mother Teresa

Printed in the United States
by Baker & Taylor Publisher Services